THE MANAGER'S GUIDE
TO HUMAN BEINGS

Understanding our human nature at work

Bronach Crawley

First published 2019 by
Bouncing Books
Maltings, 1 Knoll Wood, Godalming
GU7 2EW
England

+44 (0)1483 418901

First published 2019

A CIP catalogue record for this book is available
from the British Library.

ISBN-13: 978-0-9930212-3-7

Typesetting by
Chandlerbookdesign.com

About the Author
Bronach Crawley BSC PhD MPhil MSc

For over thirty-five years, Bronach Crawley has worked as a psychologist in the commercial world and the public sector. Trained in both clinical and occupational psychology, she has a fascination with how individuals manage their work life and how the collective organisation behaves. She has held roles as a university lecturer and clinical psychologist at the Institute of Psychiatry, worked in career development in financial services, been an HR consultant in a major consulting firm, and run her own business, Bronach Crawley Consulting. She is currently a director of the Domino Partnership. Throughout, her interest has been, and remains, uncovering the real reasons human beings do what they do. She is a specialist in assessment, psychological profiling, facilitation, teaching consulting skills, coaching at senior levels with teams and individuals, and designing programmes to promote sustainable change. Bronach is an associate fellow of the British Psychological Society and a member of the BPS specialist group on coaching.

For my boys,
three wonderful human beings.

CONTENTS

Acknowledgements

This book would still be a jumble of thoughts languishing in my brain had it not been for the help of numerous exceptional people. A round of applause goes to Hilary Farrar, Philip Lindsay and to the inspirational Sandy Cotter who took a risk on me and transformed my academic approach into something useful. To Lawrie Philpot, who had confidence in the notion of this book so very long ago. To all my friends at YSC for allowing me to be their associate, drink their coffee and be part of their furniture for many years. Particular thanks go to Professor Patricia Bossons, Sherief Hammady, Rachel Robinson, Nik Kinley and Guy Gumbrell for their invaluable comments on earlier drafts. I am grateful to the Harvard Business Review, the CIPD and Aaron Hurst for allowing me to quote from their texts and, of course, endless thanks to Guy, Dominic, Tom and Joe just for being you.

Introduction

P eople are people regardless of where they are and what they do, whether they are tending to the needs of the sick, figuring out finances or selling clothes on the high street. Putting robots, computers and buildings aside, the environment in which we earn our crust is made up of other human beings (whether leaders, subordinates, managers, clients, customers, shareholders, suppliers, patients, ombudsmen, legislators and every name you can think of) and, whenever human beings come together, interesting human being things happen. What's more, while the technical nature of a role challenges us on a range of fronts, the majority of our difficulties at work are centred on people. Human beings can be the highlight of work but they can also be the root of pain, as in pain in the backside.

Throughout my career, I have been fascinated by how much time is taken struggling with people issues when we are awash with information to help us. The books on psychological theories, management techniques, neuropsychology and emotional intelligence fill libraries. We have management development initiatives, leadership programmes and coaching coming at us from all angles. We work in an environment of people. We are people ourselves. Surely, accounting for the human being aspects of work should be like falling off a log, that easy, but somehow, it just isn't.

Recognising and managing people as human beings is a tall order for many reasons. Surprisingly, the very systems and processes that are supposed to help us in this quest can easily lead towards further misunderstanding and confusion. It seems that the more we attempt to systemise and categorise our understanding of people through sophisticated Human Resources (HR) methodologies, the further we seem to be from recognising the human being within each of us. I hold my hand up here because those of us on the inside of HR have much to account for. We have created an industry with tools and techniques that promise much but which often oversimplify and thereby mislead. We have suggested to managers that the burden of difficult human being tasks can be lifted and placed elsewhere.

Yet, it isn't possible to outsource the responsibility for managing people to techniques, systems, other functions or other organisations because real people management takes place within every interaction we make. It consists of the everyday world of contact between human beings, the *us* and the *them* and, make no mistake, it's as much about *us* as it is about *them*. If you're a manager, it's about you and your people. So, it's time to face up to it: managing human beings is difficult but it's also the stuff of real life, every single day.

Beyond this, we have been so keen, or perhaps so browbeaten, to align ourselves to the financial drivers of business strategy that we have lost touch, literally, with the individual human beings that are the living cells that create a living organisation. We have also chosen to pay only minimal heed to the purpose of organisations as entities that serve all stakeholders, that is, all the human beings affected by an organisation's actions whether directly or at the end of a lengthy chain of events. In the long term, this organisational blindness begins to erode the foundations on which an organisation exists and may, in part, explain why corporate lifespan has shortened considerably over the past century, with average longevity now below that expected for a human being[1] and with many not even reaching adolescence. Certainly, organisations appear and disappear for a variety of reasons but forgetting the impact of human nature on organisational life seems to wield a critical injury.

> ... there is currently evidence that corporations fail because of the prevailing thinking and language of economics. To put it another way: Companies die because their managers focus on the economic activity of producing goods and services, and they forget that their organizations' true nature is that of a community of humans. The legal establishment, business educators and the financial community all join them in this mistake.
>
> De Geus, The Living Company (2002)[2]

If ignoring the human element is a risky and potentially damaging business, the need for an alternative is self-evident. We can only foster a true understanding of how we humans operate by putting human being, rather than human resource, issues high on the organisational agenda. By consciously working with, rather than against, our nature, we will be better placed to harness the power of motivated people, using their talents and energy to bring innovation and commitment to a common purpose. This can only be a good thing and it's what this book is about.

So, whether you manage people on a small or large scale, I hope that by reminding you of what matters to you, to your family, friends, colleagues and all those you encounter in your work life, you will see beyond their title or associated performance indicators, to meet them as human to human and reap the rewards of your effort.

The style of this book

If you are holding a paper copy of this book, you will have noticed that it's a slim volume. Strangely, it started as a much longer, rather academic book but as I learned more it shrank. What study and, more importantly, experience have taught me is that the most valuable lessons that help in our dealings with other people fall into the category of straightforward common sense. Unfortunately, in our quest to become more sophisticated operators (and to make money out of HR), simple ideas that don't need a training course or a certificate before they can be applied have often been overlooked. Understanding these basic concepts matters because, if we are to build meaningful ways of helping people give of their best, we need to get the foundations right. By stripping away peripheral HR speak and going back to human being first principles, we have a greater chance of getting to grips with the fundamental issues that affect the way we work. These principles are not difficult to grasp. As a member of the human race, you are already familiar with them even if you may not have considered some of them before in the context of work.

The chapters that follow are intended to remind you of these human being basics. They do not provide a new theory, a fixed framework or a set of rigid processes. Instead, they suggest simple guidelines, questions and prompts to help you explore your approach to the human beings you work with, whatever the environment, role or level you occupy. If, however, you have a craving for facts, figures and references, I suggest you turn to the aforementioned libraries for a deeper immersion in the world of psychology. When you have distilled the information you read there, I trust you will find considerable overlap with the issues raised in this volume.

Hints on how to use this book

Starting from the premise that we are all different, I assume that every reader will approach this book in their own way, so my guidance on how to use it is, I hope, wide enough to allow for us all.

- Firstly, as you read each chapter, consider how the content relates to you. Use yourself as a specimen to be examined, looked at from top to bottom and from inside out. Consider how you operate at work and at home. Spot the differences. What do you find easy and what do you struggle with? Which parts of your human being nature are being addressed, allowing you to work freely from your strengths? Which parts are being neglected, leaving an unhelpful imprint on the way you operate?

- Secondly, think about the members of your team or those around you in your world of work. Relate the concepts raised to particular people and/or incidents in the workplace to help ground what you read. Although the material in this book is, in many respects, simple and straightforward to grasp, it is extraordinarily rich in terms of its implications. Don't rush ahead because the text is easy to read. Take your time to ask what the content means to the unique human beings you know.

- Thirdly, make a note, mentally or physically of the matters that jump out at you, shouting from the page. These are most likely to be the issues that are of specific importance to you and that need further consideration whether that involves lone thinking time, discussion over coffee with friends or colleagues, half an hour on the internet to garner more information, or serious help.

- Then create your own laboratory. Experiment with changing the way you operate. We do not work in a vacuum and any change you make will create ripples, or maybe even a tidal wave, that could prompt a significant difference in others. You might try some of the suggestions provided or devise fascinating investigations of your own. Whatever you do, please allow yourself to make mistakes along the way. After all, you're only human.

A word on terminology. Frequently, I refer to 'we' rather than 'you'. That's because I'm human too and the issues raised on the following pages are about us all, including me. To avoid the awkward s/he split, I use *he* because it's shorter than typing *she*. Absolutely no sex-role stereotyping is intended whatsoever. And I do mean whatsoever.

This book has taken over a quarter of a century to travel from idea to reality. Along the way, I have had the opportunity to meet many delightful people who have been willing to share something of their human being self with me. For this, I am extremely grateful. It has made the journey a fascinating and enjoyable adventure.

Bronach Crawley

CHAPTER 1

What Makes Us Human?

W e are all human beings. Hard to believe but it's a fact. The evil boss, the bully of a teacher who made your life hell and even the embarrassing relative with the worst shoes in the world – yes, they are human too. Like us, they share defining characteristics that set us apart from other animals. From the numerous programmes on the natural world, every TV viewer knows that *Homo sapiens* (from wise man) evolved from primates. We are so closely related that the genus *Pan* (common chimpanzees and bonobos) shares 99% of our DNA, which could explain a lot about the shoes.

If we look inside a human being, what do we find? The answer to this depends on what we're looking for. A medical student could choose a simple physical examination to understand the basic anatomy of a person. He might also make use of blood tests or an X-ray to gain a different perspective. With enough budget, he could use the wonders of modern technology to examine his willing subject using sophisticated scans. The individual could be sliced (metaphorically) laterally, horizontally or on the diagonal by an MRI or CT scan. One area could be examined in minor detail or pictures could be created for the whole body. The individual could be viewed in a static state or in the process of his 'engine running' through a PET scan, and so on. In each case, what the medical student sees would depend on where and how he chooses to look.

The psychologist is no different. What he sees depends on what 'slice' of an individual he puts under his psychological microscope. If I ask Mr X to complete a psychometric measure with only four major dimensions today then use another with eighteen the next day, the data I gather will be different but Mr X remains the same. In a coaching session, if I choose to talk about behaviour only and do not look at the causes of the behaviour, I will see the behaviour only. If I choose to talk about cause without discussing the implications of the causes, I will gain a detailed insight into the individual's thinking structure and feelings but will have less understanding of their impact on his everyday life.

Where we look influences what we see. The key to understanding human beings is to ensure that we look in the right place. So, let's start with a few obvious pointers.

We think and we feel

We may share much of our DNA with chimpanzees but we are a long way apart in terms of our capability. At any number of stages, evolution might have thrown us along a different path but it did not. We are as we are, walking upright, with highly developed brains, using complex language and speech, capable of fine actions with our hands and organising ourselves into groups and societies of many forms. What smart creatures we are. In combination, our brains, our language and our physical abilities allow us to manipulate our world, and each other, in extraordinary ways. The extent of this manipulation is made possible by the development of the brain's cortex which has given us the ability to use thought and imagination to play with our view of the world; thoughts and language are tools with which we imagine possibilities, analyse problems, plan for the future, reflect on the past and think about 'me'. Then, if we choose, we can share this inner world with others. Our ability to reflect and to think about our thinking allows for huge leaps in learning.

But, and it is a big but, we are not as modern and enlightened as we may wish to believe. We carry with us evidence of the evolutionary trail through which we developed, beyond a redundant appendix.

Before we had conscious thought to play with, our predecessors' lives were driven to a considerable extent by more primitive reactions where a stimulus led to a simple physiological sensation. In more complex beings, these sensations, or feelings, became linked to a thought of some kind and began their journey as a means of deep rooted influence on behaviour. At the top of the evolutionary tree, we humans call feelings 'emotions'. The fact that we can use our thinking skills to label, discuss and write PhD theses on emotions does not mean that we have left behind their influence on our decision-making. Certainly not. Our emotions are with us at every moment of every day, exerting a powerful influence on the path we follow, even if we are unaware of it at times.

We think and we feel – a simple fact, not rocket science, but strangely often overlooked in the world of work. What's more, we do not think or feel in isolation. Our thoughts and our feelings are deliciously intertwined. The mind, the seat of thoughts, and the body, in large part the home of our feelings, operate as one system. Kick one and the other jumps.

We operate on many levels

Many folk, including the delightful film character Shrek, have noted that there is more to human beings (and ogres) than a surface examination suggests. Like an onion, if we keep peeling layers away, we find more underneath. Each human layer can be subdivided and divided again but to help us in our quest for simplicity I will focus on four major divisions.

- **Behaviour:** action that we can see (so it's easy to spot) but there's an awful lot of it (so it's challenging to understand).

- **Styles and preferences:** how we like to operate; general trends that influence subsections of our behaviour.

- **Values and beliefs:** our fundamental views on life, often shaped by our early years and significant experiences.

- **Core human needs:** what matters to us all.

These layers are built on top of each other rather like a trifle – with the cake and fruit at the bottom followed by some jelly on which custard floats, topped with a line of cream – but with one big difference. These layers are permeable.

In human beings, what lies at our core influences our values and beliefs, our preferences and ultimately our behaviour. That would be like the raspberries at the base of my trifle dish rising into the jelly then into the custard until they mingle with the whipped cream at the top. In our human trifle, each layer is affected by the layers beneath it, either directly, as in a counselling session when we may be asked to talk about what matters most to us in life, or indirectly, in the choices we make each day.

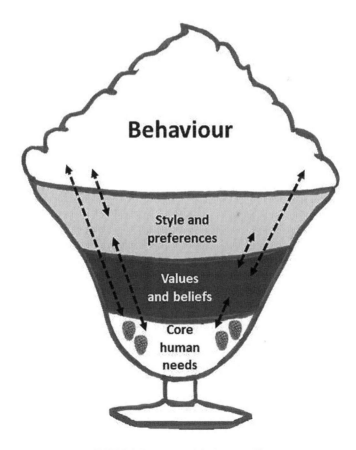

FIGURE 1: The layers of the human trifle

Not to overcomplicate matters, but we can't leave out the fact that the arrows also flow the other way. What happens in our environment, either directly to us or around us, can affect all layers to a greater or lesser degree. For example, the way my boss treats me can reinforce or challenge the view I have of myself. The way politicians behave can make me shift my political beliefs. The closer I come to personal tragedy, the more I may question my values, and so on.

What determines how the layers interact is down to our genes, the environment and the experiences we encounter in life. Genes influence the layers because the nature of the fruit, custard, jelly or cream can vary. What we start with in terms of temperament and neurological potential will influence how we interact with our environment. Then the environment and our history of experiences play their part. To stretch an analogy to its utmost limits, a trifle left in the sun might get very runny and the fruit might float to the top easily. A trifle left in the fridge might become a more solid barrier to movement. Enough before we're all sick.

The layers analogy reminds us that to understand how human beings operate, we need to consider more than the surface actions. To understand behaviour, we must look deeper to find the *why*. Anyone who has parented, taught or looked after a teenager will know just what I mean. On the surface, some behaviour just doesn't make sense.

We have a fifth layer: neuroscience and the brain

The past twenty-five years have been exciting times for the human brain. Having remained the most mysterious organ of our being throughout our evolutionary history, the brain is, at last, beginning to yield its secrets for us to share. With the aid of modern technology, neuroscientists are now able to watch as the brain goes into action, translating physical events and thoughts into detectible responses in brain tissue. Neuroscience has given us another, fifth, layer to examine. It has allowed us to understand more accurately the impact of damage to the brain. By illuminating the way in which different areas of the brain work together, it has shown us the physiological events that occur as we go about our business. These advances have the potential to do more than explain what's going on inside our skulls. In some instances, they indicate how different interventions may influence the way in which our brains respond. Undoubtedly, in years to come, greater awareness of how the brain functions will lead to significant advances in the management of neurological ill health and, further, will allow us to maximise the impact of a healthy brain. Yet, in most cases, understanding the complex brain activity underlying our thought processes isn't necessary in order to change the way we think and feel. Human beings already have the capacity to do that without understanding the fine detail of the fifth layer. Our ability to think about our thinking and to think about our feeling gives us the power to create change.

We have parts of our being we do not know

The interaction between thought and emotion can be highly complex. How dull life would be if it wasn't. For a start, both can occur at a conscious level – we may know that we are unhappy and we may know the reasons why. They can also occur at a subconscious level. Think snakes, a person who jumps out before you in a dark alley or whatever scares the pants off you. In moments of extreme fear, our emotional and physiological reactions kick in before conscious thought gets anywhere near processing what's going on. Think too of how the elusive answer to a crossword puzzle appears apparently out of nowhere when you left the puzzle behind many hours ago and had not given a moment's conscious thought to it since. Surprise, surprise, your brain was working away at that puzzle without you even noticing. The Nobel Prize winner Daniel Kahneman[3] describes this fascinating aspect of our being as 'system 1' thinking: thinking that is conducted out of our awareness, automatically, with little or no effort and with no sense of voluntary control. In contrast, 'system 2' thinking occurs when we consciously pay attention to a task or thought. It requires effort, tends to be slower, is based on rational analysis and is the thinking we are most familiar with because it happens in conscious awareness. In other words, we know it's going on because we focus on it. Most of us assume it's the only thinking going on. Yet how wrong we are.

Our level of awareness has several significant implications.

- If we know what we are doing and why, we have the choice to continue or to alter our behaviour.

- If we know what we're doing but do not know why, or have an incorrect reasoning of why, our choices for change are limited.

- If we don't know what we're doing in the first place, we're either in a state of denial or drunk as a skunk. Whichever, we are vulnerable to the vagaries of the situation.

This means that, in the world of work, where managers and leaders want their staff to perform in particular ways, simply instructing people to change may not be enough. The wise manager considers the 'why' question. Why would people do what I want them to do? More importantly, why wouldn't they? A wiser manager would recognise that this is not as simple as 'because it's their job'.

We are unique works of art

You may or may not be a fan of Sigmund Freud, the father of psychoanalysis, but, whatever your views on potty training, we should all be grateful to the Austrian psychoanalyst for pointing out that our early experiences are particularly important in shaping the person we grow to be. There is nothing mystical about this view. You will accept, I'm sure, that when we're wriggling around in nappies our brains still have much to do in the way of development before we can become competent adults. Consider too that what we experience early on goes into our memory against a fairly clean backdrop. The brain, however, is a disciplined organ and likes to have everything in its place. It doesn't just throw the traces of our experiences into a mental sack all jumbled up. The brain is self-organising – it seeks to build a personalised framework on which it can hang the memory of later experiences. This unique and ever-evolving framework becomes our guide to how the world works, an appreciation of cause and effect – *when this happens, the result is X; when that happens, the result is Y*. As our early experiences form the first bones of this framework, they help determine how the memory of later experiences will be ordered: whether they confirm or contradict the framework.

Importantly, this framework is more than a mental filing cabinet. It provides guidance on *where* to put our focus next – the direction in which we then choose to look. For example, if a young child's first encounter with a dog is a snarling animal baring its teeth, he may add to his framework the belief that 'all dogs are dangerous'. From that point onwards, the child may then refuse to go near any dog, focusing foremost on the sharp teeth and unpredictable behaviour of the animal. Hence, he does not learn that dogs can also be loving, fun and harmless. Drawn to notice the teeth in other animals, his fear of dogs may then widen to cats, horses and all other sharp-toothed beings. Another child, whose first encounter with a dog is with a small, soft and friendly animal, adds to his framework the belief that dogs are not harmful. Whenever he sees a dog, he doesn't notice the dog's teeth but pays attention to the animal's warm fur and wagging tail. He interacts with a wide range of dogs and other animals without fear even when he is old enough to know that animals can, on occasion, bite. The framework created by each child is different and alters not only their choice of subsequent activity but also what they see, think and feel about it. It is in this way that our attention becomes selective, affecting how further frameworks are shaped. Consequently, our journey of growing up becomes highly individual. Even if we follow the same path as other people, our interpretation of what we see on that path will be unique.

As we get older and more self-aware, experience hones or challenges our mental frameworks and we have greater conscious choice about how we see the world. We can become the architects of new frameworks for our thinking, choosing what we want to believe, to store or to throw out. Yet, against all this awareness, our early frameworks are not erased. They still bubble away, influencing our thoughts, even though the beliefs that underpin them and their origins are likely to be hidden from our conscious thinking. And some of these old frameworks can be extremely potent. It's a little like running a program on a computer over which we think we have full control, unaware that there's another, much older, program running out of sight that's interfering with the commands we make.

An adult with a fear of animals in unlikely to recall that he encountered a snarling dog at the age of eighteen months as few of us can access memories from our preschool years. Childhood amnesia, as it's known, means that it is rare to remember events from before the first three to four years of life.[4] We don't know what our early frameworks might have been and, mostly, we can chug along nicely without being bothered by this blind spot. But, if we hit difficult times, for example undue depression, anxiety, lack of self-confidence, performance problems at work, difficulty in maintaining relationships and so on, we may need to get to grips with the underlying (and potentially outdated) framework that may be interfering with our well-being. Sometimes, other family members and friends can provide illuminating information about early experiences allowing us to hypothesise what might have shaped our thinking and feeling. Sometimes we just have to guess.

We are unique but we share common attributes

Although we are all unique and see the world in unique ways, we do share common attributes, like the notion of layers, core needs etc. If we didn't, there would be no point in this book and your role as a manager of people would be extremely difficult. There would also be a very long queue of psychologists, therapists and counsellors at the jobcentre door. Fortunately, human beings have enough in common to allow us to create a language to examine our human condition. We use these commonalities to guide us to an area on which to focus and then look for individual differences within it. In this book, I present one such language but you have many others to choose from. Whichever you eventually alight upon to guide your practice as a manager, please don't lose sight of the fact that common patterns only point us in a general direction of investigation in our quest of understanding the exquisite uniqueness of each other.

Why do we need to know this human being stuff?

Human beings are capable of acts of heroism, altruism, generosity, kindness, creativity, genius and more. We are also capable of a litany of evil and a wide range of plain mediocre in-between. When we have a better understanding of our make-up as human beings, we have greater conscious control over our thoughts and our feelings. We are in the driving seat. Then, provided the environment allows us to do so, we have the choice to use our potential to the full. Sometimes, even when the environment is against us, we find the strength and courage to change our circumstances and free our potential.

To help people achieve this, our approach to living with, supporting or managing humankind requires a willingness to think in more than one dimension, down through the different layers of our being. This is tricky, too tricky for the majority of HR initiatives. Most take an easier way out by emphasising only one or two layers (most notably behaviour and style). This 'Flat Stanley'[5] approach is fine in its way as it yields manageable data but grave errors are made when it is assumed that one perspective gives the whole story. For example, two people may produce identical profiles on a set of psychometric measures but they will not be identical people or behave in identical ways. At an organisational level, if managers rely on partial data and yet believe it tells the full story, mistakes will be made.

At an individual level, psychological maturity comes from knowing ourselves better, becoming aware of the parts of us that lurk in the hidden layers of the human trifle dish, hypothesising about ourselves when we have no data to go on, and appreciating the mental frameworks on which we run. Whether we then use this awareness for good or bad is up to us but my hope is that it's for the former. Learning to manage people well is as much about understanding ourselves as it is about understanding those who work for, with and around us. Sorry, but there it is. So, when you read on, think not about *them* but about *us*. How can you understand more of your human being self in order to help the human beings in your own particular world?

What next?

The interwoven nature of thinking and feeling in the human condition has many consequences. Getting to grips with these consequences is an important key in unlocking our understanding of people. Therefore, it's to emotion and thinking that we turn next.

CHAPTER 2

We Are Heart and Computer

A t work, most of us like to think that we deal with the overt tasks placed before us using logical reasoning. We assume that our decisions arise from a rational appreciation of the facts before us with our emotional selves left firmly at home. Even if we are in the caring professions, although we use our emotions to support and understand others, when it comes to decision-making we choose to believe that we do this in a dispassionate way. However, can we compartmentalise our human being nature so easily? The answer has to be a clear 'no'.

There are some things that go with us everywhere, that we cannot leave at home and that will almost certainly be with us on that crowed train journey or in the long traffic jam as we travel to work. They make themselves comfortable on the seats we hang our jackets on and are a watchful presence as we choose the cheese bagel over the salad for lunch. Whether we like it or not, we cannot leave our core beliefs, our values, our feelings and our personalities behind. Our behaviour may bob along on the surface but the other layers of our human being self are not very far away. They run through us like the letters in a stick of rock.

'But what about Attila H. over there? He's the most heartless, cold, unemotional manager I've ever met,' I hear a chorus cry. We've all met a few of those but don't confuse an individual's lack of compassion or overt emotion at work, a preference for profit before people, or even a display of cruel behaviour as meaning that the emotional self has been left in the locker room. Usually, this type of behaviour is provoked by emotion even if the individual concerned is blind to its influence. Not showing emotion does not mean emotions are absent.

Is emotion wrong?

Emotion may be painful or joyous to experience, or anywhere in-between, and the behaviour that flows from it may be desirable or less desirable, depending on your standpoint. Despite many cultural norms that suggest overt displays of emotion at work are in some way wrong, emotion itself is neither good nor bad. It just is. It's also a misconception to say that emotion is illogical. When we make decisions based on our underlying emotional needs, we are often just as logical as when we are not but we are applying that logic in a different way. It's like taking the same set of data and dropping it into an equation about emotion rather than the overt equation we might appear to be considering.

Life without emotion is unimaginable. There would be no colour, no taste, no complexity, no humanity. Fortunately, emotion is a sticky thing. It won't give us up easily. We can't ask human beings not to bring their emotion to work. It simply isn't possible. Yet, traditionally in the Western world we have honoured cool, intellectual logic and dismissed emotion as an interfering and unbusinesslike force to be dealt with by the nice people in HR.

This is, perhaps, simply an excuse for avoiding something we don't understand but all the avoidance in the world isn't going to make emotion disappear, even at work. It's here to stay and it's time we gave greater recognition to the power of our emotional selves. Not to do so is simply delusion.

The heart and computer model

To aid our understanding of emotion, there is one simple rule that we have first to grasp. Think on this:

- for shorthand, consider the logical, analytical, thinking part of our being to be like a *computer*;

- call the emotional, belief-based, physiological processing part the *heart*;

- appreciate that decisions are influenced by both our heart and computer (our emotion and our reasoning);

BUT (and here's the rule)

- remember that we use them in that order – heart before computer.

That's it. Remember nothing else from here on and that should be enough to make a difference.

When I take information in, say listening to another person talking or when I'm reading a newspaper, I run it first through my 'heart'. I probably don't know I'm doing this but it's happening all the same. The heart acts like a filter. It checks the information for anything that might relate to me personally. The closer the link to my own circumstances and its potential to affect my well-being, the stronger the reaction (the emotion) created in response, whether consciously or subconsciously. The heart's filter checks not only for issues of immediate relevance (e.g. things that could affect a female middle-aged psychologist living in Surrey) but also for anything I value or hold strong feelings about (e.g. my family, my politics, my football team, my religion, my nationality). The heart, then, acts as a first decision point to determine if the information coming in is potentially good or bad for me. It catches a more fundamental meaning in what might otherwise be a random series of transactions. It links the immediate, here and now, to a deeper sense of 'me'.

My heart may share some aspects with yours but it will not be the same as we each have our own individual set of filters. Made up from the leftover fragments of my history, filters are a tapestry of my past emotional experiences (from my first framework and beyond) sewn onto my genetic template. In effect, a filter is the sum of the hidden layers described earlier – my beliefs, values, preferences and core values. These hidden levels hold our lives together by giving a structure on which events can be arranged and evaluated at an emotional level.

When the heart has done its bit, information gets passed on to the 'computer', along with the initial interpretation the heart has construed, where it is then analysed with logical reasoning, imagination and all the complex intellectual processing that human beings have developed. The computer is cool and unemotive. It deals factually with what's before it.

Of course, this model is an oversimplification. Our logical and emotional reasoning does not go in one straight line like a train journey where we start at A, maybe make a few stops and then arrive at B. Our decision-making is made up of a constant interaction between our emotion and our logical thought. It is a journey where we change direction, revisit places, stop altogether or change mode of transport, weaving our way along a path. A discussion over a difficult matter with your boss may start off in a heated way but be easily defused by some information, moving into a more factual debate until he says something that touches a raw nerve and your emotional processing reframes the situation once more. Despite this, the essence of this model still holds true. Heart comes before computer, meaning that our inner emotional make-up impacts on how we interpret the world about us and how we apply subsequent rational thought.

The consequences of heart first

Pseudo-logic can rule: When our emotions are tinkering with us but we don't know it, we risk acting without full control over our behaviour. We may be blind to the true reasons for what we're doing. However, our logical computer does not like this 'not knowing'. Where a reason is absent, it will create one. Unless it has been trained to do so (as a therapist is), the computer rarely detects the hidden emotional drivers at play. Instead, it generates its own ideas to provide a reasonable explanation for our behaviour. It finds a 'good enough' explanation without having to call on a deeper motive. This is *unintentional pseudo-logic*. Because it's generated by our computer, it looks like logic, it smells like logic and it sounds like logic and it may well be backed up with facts but it's not centred on what is really driving the behaviour at core. Sometimes, this is fine and it doesn't matter a jot. Sometimes it's highly destructive. Here's an example that might help explain it.

Logical ping-ping: A group of senior executives sit around a table debating a key issue. Each has his own perspective on the matter. One individual shoots an idea onto the table but it's batted back by another with a logical reason for why it will not work. The idea is then shot back nicely with a reason for why it will. A flaw in this reasoning allows a nifty backhand to spin the idea right back where it started. The meeting continues in this way until a killer point is scored and the others give up through boredom, exhaustion or when one player, usually the most senior, pulls out a giant-sized bat and waves it around a little for effect. Get my drift? What's really going on? If the group want to achieve the best answer, they would surely build a solution together, maybe extracting good points from the different opinions offered. Instead, they compete. In this instance, the real drive fuelling the exchange is the need to look good in front of the chief executive and its corollary – the fear of looking like a loser in front of him – but it has been dressed up to look like an analytical debate.

What about when our motives for behaviour are not so hidden? There are certainly times when we are at least partially aware of the deeper motives for our actions although we knowingly disguise them. Then, we are employing *intentional pseudo-logic*.

The collusion game: A group of senior managers is waiting outside the office of the CEO. While they wait, they discuss several of the issues on the agenda for the meeting they are about to attend. They talk freely, all joining in at various points. The door opens and they are ushered inside. The CEO starts the meeting. The mood of the group changes significantly. The senior managers say little. They do not offer the ideas discussed earlier. They do not challenge. They talk only to the CEO, not to each other. The meeting ends with all decisions taken by the CEO, who is deeply frustrated by the performance of his team. When asked why they contributed so little, the managers all give logical arguments to support their actions in the order of 'it's the way the CEO likes to operate' (which it clearly isn't), 'it makes for a smoother running meeting' (for smoother, read shorter). Sometime later and after a review of their behaviour, each manager acknowledges that they were, in fact, afraid of the CEO and did not want to risk being humiliated in front of him or their colleagues. It was safer to say little, a ploy in which they all knowingly colluded.

In some instances, even the attempt at disguise is minimal – everyone knows the real issues at stake even though they are played out in a pseudo-logical framework. The game is on!

The power struggle: After a difficult merger between two organisations, three directors and a junior manager discuss a paper proposing a new process for promoting senior staff. This is the third such meeting and the third suggested process. One of the directors and the junior manager (who is charged with designing the system) come from the organisation deemed to be less powerful in the merger. The two other directors, who are the decision makers for the promotion process, come from the more powerful side. Once more, the decision makers provide logical reasons to reject the paper, despite the process suggested being best practice. Why is it rejected? The logic they give is not flawed but it isn't balanced. The real issue at play is the power struggle between the directors *(we're not having any of your ideas because we're in charge now)*. The 'game' is obvious through the language used, the cursory look at the papers presented, the absence of alternative suggestions, and the posturing of all three directors. They all play knowingly but the junior manager is on the sidelines and unfortunately also on the receiving end of the workload. He's had enough. 'Sort out who is in charge before asking me to waste any more of my time', he says before taking his papers and marching out. His intervention, though carrying significant personal risk, embarrassed the directors sufficiently to make them address the real issue they were avoiding. 'Playing the game' kept the directors in a loop of 'move' and 'countermove' that couldn't take the organisation forward. Dealing with the power issue openly took the directors out of that loop, enabling them to agree a solution and find a way of working together in the future.

Pseudo-logic, whether used consciously or through lack of awareness, is a huge time-waster and rarely achieves the best solution. It is endemic in our organisations because the need for achievement, to win, is prevalent at senior levels (see Chapter 9 for more on this). Masquerading as intellectual argument, pseudo-logic is frequently used as the weapon of choice to fight for the top dog position while rewarding contribution made through open collaboration is rare.

Pseudo-logic looks good and, worryingly, it's what we have come to accept as normal but is it acceptable that a good deal of serious business debate is, in fact, posturing and acting out of more personal matters with or without awareness? There are examples where organisations have collapsed as the result of foolish decisions made by a senior team: when a collective groupthink, based on the pseudo-logic of business advantage, led an organisation swiftly towards the compost heap of history; when the drive for short-term self-aggrandisement or financial reward for the few got the better of the true logic of a situation. Many leaders and managers have much to learn if they are to understand how to build new ideas rather than apply an intellectual bulldozer to leave the strongest standing.

A word of caution. Do not feel you are immune to the effects of hidden drives and pseudo-logic. It's part of being human. We all fall victim to its charm.

Filters can become blocked: If an event causes a significant emotional reaction, our emotional filters may get blocked. This slows down the rate at which data is passed through to the computer. Imagine a giant coffee filter. A small amount of ground coffee allows the water to pass through relatively quickly. Pack the coffee machine to the brim with compressed coffee and the flow is slowed down. The logical brain may not have time to wait for the reduced flow of data to reach it. For example, you may have told me some news that made me reel inside but you want an answer about it now. What I say in the heat of the moment may not be fully thought through because I am busy working on the emotional business the news has created. In these instances, my overt logical analysis will be skewed because it is based on partial data. The appraisal meeting is a classic situation where this arises.

> **Why doesn't he get it?** A manager has some difficult yet justifiable feedback to give to his staff member in a performance appraisal. He's done his training so he knows to give the good news first, then areas for improvement with plenty of factual examples. His appraisee appears to listen. He agrees with the facts given but finds reasons why the resulting problems were not his fault. The manager tries again, rephrasing the information, emphasising the positive and giving more examples about what needs to change. The appraisee rejects the areas for improvement more strongly, stating that the manager only ever sees the negative, then goes into a sulk. The meeting ends on a frosty note. The manager cannot understand why this intelligent individual will not accept the facts. A week later, the manager tries again. This time, the appraisee not only talks calmly about the information but he presents his own plans about how he can improve.
>
> Why did the appraisee forget the positive comments? Why did he reject concrete evidence? Why the sulk? We can't know exactly because we don't know the unique emotional filters of this individual but we can guess that the manager's negative comments created an emotional reaction that caused some of the information to get 'stuck'. As a consequence, the individual ceased to hear the good news. His computer was working on partial data

while his heart was working overtime. When the emotional reaction waned, the complete feedback passed through the heart's filters to reach the computer where it was dealt with from a cooler, more balanced perspective.

The off-switch may be triggered: At times, an emotional reaction may be so strong that the information about a situation doesn't reach the computer at all. It gets stuck on one side of the filter in a torrent of emotion even if this emotion is not displayed. It's almost impossible to think rationally when in a state of extreme anger, distress or euphoria. That's why it's not a good idea to make life-changing decisions at such moments. Extreme emotion is not necessarily a bad thing, though. A high emotional state may enable us to draw on ideas that we couldn't reach when in a cooler state, allowing us to think the unthinkable, perhaps. Taking away the sobering control of our computer, although unsettling, can unleash a burst of creativity. The extraordinary talent that many famous comedians, artists and writers have accessed when in the grip of heightened emotion reminds us that the power of this emotion can be a freeing force. Alas, such intense emotion is also likely to disable our ability to consider the implications of our ideas and to discriminate between the good and the bad. Again, with time, emotion often settles sufficiently to allow the computer 'on button' to be activated and more factual analyses carried out. In his discussion of emotional intelligence, Daniel Goleman[6] talks about 'emotional hijacking' – when an instinctive response cuts in before logical thinking arrives on the scene. When I see a large black spider scurrying across my kitchen floor, I scream before I remind myself that it is more afraid of me than

I am of it. After my initial outburst, my computer provides the information needed to calm me which, in turn, allows me to take action to remove the spider (with the aid of a glass and card of course). Overruling an instinctive response is not easy. It's taken several decades to allow my computer to dampen the shriek of fear when I see eight hairy legs running towards me.

Our processor may malfunction: In extreme situations, where the emotional pain caused by an event may be too damaging for an individual to cope with, the computer can be corrupted. This is beyond the filter being selective in what it allows through. It's as though the computer has been infected with a nasty emotional virus that infiltrates the software of our thinking. Having done so, the virus alters incoming information in a fundamental way. The individual still thinks he is processing data logically without being aware that the programme is distorting reality. Although rare, this distortion can serve a valuable, protective purpose when reality is too hard to face. It may be the only way of coping with a traumatic event. Consider victims of abuse who blame themselves for the actions of an abuser when the facts are clearly the opposite. This is particularly the case with children who are abused by their parents. They often remain loyal to the people who are hurting them, seeing themselves as deserving of the abuse, because it's too agonising to acknowledge that those who should love and protect them are the cause of their pain. Abusers, too, often find logic in their actions. History is littered with examples of cruelty excused by the perpetrators as 'I was just following the orders of my superiors' because to acknowledge their own responsibility would be emotionally devastating. Although such erroneous logic provides a way out from facing pain in extreme circumstances, it usually creates other problems in its wake. When emotion is repressed, it doesn't pack its bags and leave. It stays at a subconscious level, potentially distorting an increasing spectrum of information. Research on the long-term and highly damaging effects of post-traumatic stress bears witness to this.[7]

How to work with both heart and computer

An essential prerequisite for the effective management of people is the recognition that human being issues, experienced and responded to through both a heart and a computer, will be of critical importance to each person we encounter whatever their role or level in, or outside, the organisation. That is, in terms of hierarchy, human being issues come before anything work can throw at us. Even if we are in our office, grafting away for every hour possible, we are doing it for a human being reason. Having a clearer perspective on what these reasons might be can only help us in our quest to enable people to give of their best. To start us off, here a few general pointers to prompt this holistic human perspective and a good place to begin is with you.

Get to know yourself better: There is more to you than meets the eye. You have psychological nooks and crannies yet to be discovered. For some of us, they may be canyons. For others, they are small, dark hollows. Whichever, we should never stop learning about ourselves. *Why do I need to know myself better? Surely, it's my staff that I need to understand*. The answer to this is straightforward. You are part of the system in which your staff exist. What they do affects you and what you do affects them. Your style impacts on their world. Your psychological clutter makes their life easier or more difficult, an enjoyable experience or hell at times. Fortunately, you don't need to be a 'perfect' manager (as perfection isn't possible) but you are required to act with a reasonable degree of awareness about your emotions. Do you know what pushes your buttons? What or who makes you feel good about yourself? What or who makes you feel bad about yourself? What and who irritates you/scares you/worries you? If you think you're never scared or worried, run that past yourself once again because it's unlikely to be the case. Increasing your awareness increases your choice of action because, instead of being driven by unknown emotional needs, you call the shots. To do so, you do not need to become a different person or undergo a lifetime of therapy. You simply need to have the courage to put the spotlight on yourself and take an honest view of what you see, highlighting both your strengths and the areas that need a little extra attention.

Become a human being detective: A good manager can reframe a task from 'how do I achieve x' to 'how do I enable my people to get to x'. This may seem obvious but, beyond setting goals and targets, sufficient attention is rarely afforded to this to make it a consistent reality. If you truly want to harness both motivation and skill to help the human beings in your team perform at their peak, you will need to think, feel and plan for more than the surface task. You will have to seek out or pick up clues that help you understand the root cause of performance issues. In short, you will need to be a human being detective. The next chapter will give you a few tips on how to do this.

Recognise emotion when it's present: If you 'just don't do emotion' you must look to yourself because, if you want to manage human beings well, you have to be able to face emotion and its implications. Ignoring emotion might get you out of tight spot but it certainly doesn't make it go away, as this example illustrates.

> John calls Alan, the most senior member of his team, into his office to explain his plans for restructuring the department to a flatter arrangement. Alan, feeling that his career prospects have been harmed by this change, says little. John is surprised by Alan's somewhat curt reaction to the news. As he wasn't expecting this response, he is unprepared for it so he carries on, giving more details about his plans and the implications for how work will now be divided among his team. He tells Alan that the plans have not been finalised; he wanted to fill Alan in first and would value his feedback. Alan still says little and the meeting ends by John asking Alan if he is happy with the plan, to which Alan says 'Fine'. Well that's ok, thinks John, as Alan leaves the room, perhaps the guy was just having an off day. Alan, feeling his own ambitions have been trampled over, shoots off several ill-advised and incorrect emails ranting about his jerk of a boss who is not giving his team any say in the future of the department.

If you're not to ignore emotion, what can you do? The *pull-yourself-together approach* (i.e. stop having this emotion in front of me) or the *box-of-tissues-there-there* method (i.e. I'll wait until it's all over and then pretend it never happened) are remarkably popular but not to be recommended. In the longer term, you will have greater success with a simple three-step approach:

1. **Spot feeling:** look and listen for reactions; focus on more than words.

2. **Bring emotion into the open:** present it as a hypothesis e.g. 'You look rather annoyed. Have I picked that up correctly? How do you feel about it?'

3. **Respect emotion:** make it clear that the reaction, whatever it may be, is valid even if it's not how you would have reacted. Respect, the R word, crops up again and again in the chapters that follow because it's the key that provides access to the human heart.

Give time for emotional processing: Time is amazing. We may feel we have too little of it but it works wonders with our emotions. In most instances, time allows us to heal because it enables our emotional filters to clear. With time, even extreme reactions calm, allowing us to examine our feelings and our behaviours and take stock. This doesn't mean that emotion disappears but more that we are no longer in the full grip of its power. When we talk of processing emotion, we mean finding ways to manage *it* rather than *it* controlling us. You may be familiar with this concept in terms of bereavement when, with time, the disabling rawness of the immediate loss of a loved one eventually fades to allow us to continue our life even though the loss may still be felt for a lifetime. In the world of emotion at work, ultimately you will save time by giving time. If you spot strong reactions, take a breathing space, even if it's just a short coffee break. When difficult messages are to be given, you may want longer; for instance, break an appraisal meeting over two days. The message is: when emotions are heightened, revisit issues at different time intervals.

Harness the power of emotion: You may think that a manager's life is hard enough, dealing with all the usual nonsense that work throws your way, without having to take account of all this human being stuff. That could be true but consider this. Perhaps your life would be easier if you did. Not only can you make interactions more straightforward by identifying what is really happening rather than colluding with the posturing that occurs from hidden needs but you can also use emotions to your advantage. When people are truly engaged with an enterprise, they care about achieving the best possible outcome. Caring produces power because we put our emotional muscle behind the things that matter to us. The excitement I feel at the possibility of reaching a goal will get me through the rough times. The disappointment I feel at not achieving what I had hoped for can be channelled into a desire to achieve it on my next attempt. Anger at unfairness can provide the fuel needed to renew effort to address the unfairness.

> *Karen's team has received some unfair public criticism due to an error made by another member of the organisation. Morale is low. The team feel beaten up. Karen holds an awayday where team members vent their frustration. She acknowledges that their feelings are justified in the most part. Then she leads them through a discussion that, in summary, goes something like this. Do you believe you do a good job? (The answer is yes.) Does your work make a*

difference to the organisation and to our clients?
(Again, the answer is yes.) Whose feedback do you
value most? (The clients'.) So, are you doing a good
job? (Yes.) Do you want to do a better job? (Yes.)
How are we going to do it? Then let's get on with it
and keep our attention on what matters to us. At the
end of the day, the team feel more buoyant. They
have not forgotten the bruised feeling that came
from the bad press but Karen has refocused their
attention and their emotion on their purpose, what
they do well and how they can do a better job. She
has given them a sense of meaning in their work and
a fresh start. Her messages will have to be reiterated
regularly to keep the momentum going and she will
have to support the few who are still stuck with their
old feelings – but that's her job.

'Computer first' is a habit and habits can be broken

Western cultures and education systems promote the use of computer over heart with the consequence that it's our habit to reach for data to understand a problem and not for the feelings that may underlie it. This is not a bad thing as our world would soon descend into chaos if we were totally in the grip of individual emotional states. However, it does not excuse putting matters of the heart into the 'too difficult' desk drawer and closing it tight. Take note. Don't be smug and think this is all easy. Most of us need a degree of re-education if we are to apply the skills of our well-trained computer to the intricacies of emotion.

What next?

To understand human beings, we need rich data. Even though we may be drowning in tasks, demands and deadlines, we must keep our internal antennas tuned and ready to detect signals of change in the people around us. It's time to find your notepad and magnifying glass. We're ready for some detective work.

CHAPTER 3

The Manager as Human Being Detective

When I was at university, the professor of my department was a follower of the great psychologist B.F. Skinner, the founder of behaviourism, so behaviourism is what we were taught. It was out with the mysterious ways of psychoanalysis and in with the observable, measurable, scientific study of behaviour. We were told that if we studied what people actually did, we could apply simple rules to either encourage or discourage their actions. When I went on to study clinical psychology, the same principles held sway. By then I, like most of my fellow students, had begun to question what we had been told. We felt cheated because we had been given only part of the picture. We knew that our thoughts, our inner life, mattered to us so, surely, they must matter to our patients too. Fortunately, not long afterwards, the pendulum began to swing back the other way and today it would be hard to find a diehard behaviourist like my old prof. Whichever theoretical model they follow, most academics now agree that it simply isn't possible to understand what people do without understanding both how they think and feel.

Like the duck peacefully gliding along the water, beneath a human being's behaviour is the psychological equivalent of two feet working like crazy – a flurry of emotional, intellectual and neurological paddling keeping everything moving. The changing face of psychology has taught us that, to get to grips with people, we need to consider each individual as a whole package where what's above water (*what* we do) relates to the layers that lie below water (the *how* and *why*). If we restrict our interest to the surface layer of behaviour only, we reduce our view of human beings to the equivalent of a mechanical duck, a machine controlled by its external environment and without the slightest capacity for self-determination. As you will appreciate, you are not a mechanical toy. You have considerable control over you.

However, you are not studying your staff and colleagues in an academic fashion. You are not a therapist or counsellor to your team and you should not seek to be one. You are a manager. Your responsibility is to help those you manage to deliver the requirements of the organisation, whatever they may be. My premise is that, to do this, you need to be 'human being smart'. You need to be a human being detective with an interest in the triad of *what*, *how* and *why* in so far as they are relevant to work. Unfortunately, as soon as you raise your psychological magnifying glass you will undoubtedly realise that gathering data of this nature is a challenging business because a human being detective has to be able to both find the information he needs and then scrutinise it for accuracy.

How to be a human being detective

First, decide it's worth doing: Let's start with the basics. Why be a human being detective at all? What's the point? Try this for a reason. If we all improve both our willingness and our ability to 'read' human beings, perhaps the world would be a better place. I can't prove this of course but if we understand each other more accurately it seems to follow that our choices will be based less on the misunderstandings that lead to conflict and more on a fuller picture of our common human needs. In so doing, we are less likely to become embroiled in our own emotional reaction to others' behaviour and more able to keep a mature, balanced perspective. So that's the moral argument.

On a more practical front, human being detective skills are essential if you are faced with people or situations like these:

- **a repeater:** a problem with one or more people that crops up again and again and again and again....;

- **a match to a fuse:** an individual who evokes a negative reaction in you or others from irritation to despair;

- **a mystery:** a team member/s with potential but they're not using it;

- **a too-comfortable zone:** an old team that's set in its ways and needs to be reinvigorated;

- **a communication impasse:** a boss or peer who doesn't understand you;

- **strangers at a party:** a new team that hasn't gelled yet;

- **energy munchers:** a team that's performing brilliantly but needs something more to keep them doing so in the long term;

- **help, I'm a stranger:** a new role with team members who don't know you;

- **all change:** a complex or awkward organisational change to manage.

Add to this anything that has the potential to cause you difficulty and involves human beings and it will probably cover most of your work (and non-work) day. Honing your skills as a human being detective can make you more influential and effective in every area of your role that involves people. That should make it worthwhile.

Use the key skill of a detective: Listen, listen and listen again.
A detective needs data and, if we know where to look, it's in rich supply. The spoken word is the obvious place to start but it's only part of the story. Words read from the page can be dry and unexciting: ask any schoolchild studying Shakespeare. Conversely, a Shakespeare play brought to life by talented actors overflows with meaning, emotion and conviction, keeping us laughing at clever wordplay or on the edge of our seats with tension. How we deliver words can change their meaning entirely and human beings constantly give away information about how they think and feel in the 'how' as well as the 'what' of language. Beyond words, all behaviour carries data and the true detective misses none of it. The trouble is that most of us aren't that good at listening or seeing. In our heads, we carry around so much of our own 'stuff' that it's difficult to make space for other people's 'stuff'.

If you want to gather the riches available, here are a few hints.

- **Register the choice of words and phrases used:**
Words are not selected at random even when we
are apparently talking on automatic pilot. Of course,
if we had to consider the choice of each word, our
conversations would take an age but that doesn't
mean our words are not directed in some way by our
inner frameworks. To pick up clues, listen to the colour
of words (the emotional tone or lack of). Hear where
the emphasis is placed. Listen for phrases that are
repeated and for words that are thrown away as though
meaning nothing. What do they suggest? The strength
or weakness of adjectives and the choice of metaphors
and comparators are forms of data telling us something
about the person using them.

- **Listen to what is not said:** Consider what a salesman
leaves out of his sales patter. It can sometimes be
the most revealing information about the product. Why
has it been left out? Has it been hidden, forgotten
or avoided, or just not crossed the individual's mind?
What is not said can give indirect pointers to priorities,
motives, interests, concerns or beliefs.

- **Spot uncontrolled energy:** The body gives off many
signals to indicate that spoken words are not giving
the full picture. One clue to look for is the leak of
uncontrolled energy. However tutored our delivery,
it's hard to keep energy in if it wants to get out.
Toes and fingers are a frequent escape route.
Remember presentations you've seen, or interviews

you've watched, where the person in front of you appears outwardly calm apart from his fingers jangling change in a pocket, drumming against a notepad or twiddling a pen. What could the hands be telling you? Can you remember talking to someone who was physically still apart from a foot jumping up and down? What is the foot saying that the rest of him is not? Watch two people talking over something important and see if you can spot where and when the energy leaks. As with all signals like this, there isn't a defined directory of interpretation (i.e. a tapping foot means...), just an indication that something else might be worth checking out.

- **Be alert to significant changes:** Anything that alters noticeably during a conversation, like the pace of delivery, skin colour, breathing rate or body posture (relaxed to more rigid or reverse) is useful data. Changes are caused by something. Maybe your remark hit home. Maybe you reminded the person of something they had forgotten. Maybe a question from ten minutes ago just came back to the individual and sparked a new idea. Who knows? The change simply tells you there is something more to consider if you want to.

- **Listen for 'ah ha' moments versus 'falling off the tongue' talk:** In everyday conversation, we exchange information, ideas, opinions that tend to *fall off the tongue*. This kind of talk is easy to access because it's at the front of our thinking and has probably been processed beforehand. Despite this, falling off the

tongue talk can still be extremely important, for example
when vital decisions are passed on, but it's unlikely to
have touched new ground. Appraisal meetings can be
like this. They repeat information known to both parties
but often don't get to the heart of why behaviour has
occurred. In contrast, *ah ha* moments are when a new
thought has been created, when something that was
bubbling away out of our conscious awareness pops
its head up and is recognised. Ah ha! The new thought
might confirm something you've guessed at previously
but, now it's in the open, you can work with it. Ah ha
moments are rare. They take time to reach and they
need to come from the individual himself. You can't
supply someone with an *ah ha* moment but you can ask
questions that help them arrive at it, recognising that
'it' may not be where you thought they were headed at
all.

- **Watch eyes:** What message do the individual's eyes
  give you (steely, hard, soft, open, timid, sad)? A good
  way to read eyes is to register the effect they have
  on you. See if you can label the feeling they evoke.
  Are the eyes congruent with the overt message?
  Notice, too, the direction of eye gaze. Looking away in
  a steady gaze (which is different from embarrassed
  avoidance of eye contact) usually indicates the person
  is thinking something through – accessing information
  that may have just moved from their unconscious
  to conscious thinking, an 'ah ha' moment perhaps,
  but not yet spoken aloud. When this happens, it is

important to give time for the individual to think, otherwise you will interrupt what could be the processing of a new thought.

Register the impact of another's words and actions on yourself: Intuition is a much-maligned sense. It's often ignored in favour of factual analysis because it's assumed that intuition comes from out of the blue in some mystical way. In fact, intuition is what occurs when thinking that's running out of our awareness creeps into our conscious thought. It's that inner voice that reacts to a trigger, or reminds us of something, or makes a situation clear or raises more questions when everything had seemed settled. Your intuition, your internal response to events, is important and contains information that can serve a human being detective well. For instance, consider the reaction the words and non-words of one of your team members evokes in you? Do they make you feel angry, confused or wanting more? Is this reaction unique to you or do you think others have it too? Being sensitive to your intuition takes practice because it requires splitting your attention simultaneously between the individual and your own reactions. In my experience, it's almost impossible to do this consistently. The trick is to pause every so often to register what your intuition might be trying to tell you at that moment.

Consider the individual as a whole and in context: We are all affected by our environment. Both our general surroundings and the immediate situation we face influence how we operate. Hence, to understand another human being's behaviour we must consider the context in which they work. What makes a person shine in one department may make them a poor performer in another. For example, if we parachute a highly creative marketeer into an actuarial firm, the fit is unlikely to be easy (and vice versa) unless the actuarial firm specifically wants someone with a different style and appreciates this difference. Similarly, to understand how one skill is used, it's important to understand how the individual's other skills are employed (the individuals' internal context), because our skills do not work in isolation either. A good human being detective is happy to deal with the complexity that a holistic view of human beings involves.

Raise hypotheses and avoid absolutes: Human beings apply their unique filters not only to what they see (behaviour) but to what they believe lies behind the behaviour, the *intention*. Applying intention is automatic. 'He looked up and down the road, like he was worried about something.' 'He offered me the largest slice of cake, which was so kind of him.' 'He asked about the client's family, showing great interest in them.' Was he worried, kind, interested? Who knows? That's our guess. However, although we can't know the absolute truth, we don't have to keep a blank head. We are free to formulate *hypotheses* ('maybe he said that because…'). A hypothesis can be tested and, when presented sensitively, can help move situations forward by prompting the individual to clarify their thinking and feeling, even if the hypothesis is completely wrong. But a word of warning. Don't fall into the trap of telling others how they think or feel as if it's fact (e.g. 'You're just upset because she did that'). No one likes to be told what they think or feel, even if you're spot-on about it. Absolutes tend to build brick walls. Instead, present your hypothesis as a suggestion with a willingness to accept that you may be wrong (e.g. I wonder if…? Does that make sense to you? It's just an idea, but what if… Do say if I'm on the wrong track but I wondered if…).

Put your own personal agenda 'on hold': A good detective needs a fully functioning computer as well as a sensitive heart so, if you find yourself in a situation that has roused your emotions, it's wise to delay detective work until you have your feelings under control and your 'computer' is functioning at its best. If you know you're wound up, find someone else to vent with before you attempt to have a calm, investigative conversation with the individual/s concerning you. To listen and hear another's agenda accurately, first you have to surrender your own list of concerns (but it's ok, it's only temporary!).

Check it out: It's not possible to adopt the rigour of a scientist when in the throes of everyday people management but, given that your judgements can have a significant impact on an individual's future career, it is important that you aim to be as accurate as possible in your detective work. Therefore:

- be sure to cast your net wide when gathering data to avoid relying on a single episode that may not be representative of an individual's behaviour;

- be wary of hearsay if the information doesn't fit with your own experience. Some witnesses have long memories and hold grudges;

- be careful that today's good performance isn't overshadowed by a problem from the past (the 'horns' effect) or that one particular success counteracts all other negatives (the 'halo' effect). In appraisal or promotion panels, it's not unusual to find a single, overpowering example used (inappropriately) as evidence for many areas.

In TV shows and books, detectives usually gather data to pass onto a third party, whoever's paying the bill. As a manager, your role is different. The primary recipient of your data should be the individual concerned. Why? Because only the individual can shed extra light on the data you've gathered. Check out the accuracy of what you've seen and heard with the person concerned.

Don't rush: What's the hurry? Take time to reflect on the data you've gathered. If you're not sure of something, go back for more data. Listen again. Human beings are the most important part of an organisation and detective work isn't accomplished in an instant. Remind yourself that time spent getting to the root of a problem can pay back handsomely in terms of more motivated and productive staff.

Making sense of human being data

Let's assume that you have gathered some rich information about the people you work with. What are you to make of it? Sadly, there is no code book of interpretation – where specific behaviours have specific intentions – whatever popular psychology texts might suggest. For instance, I cross my arms out of habit whether I'm being defensive or not. My close relatives do it too; it's a family trait. Yes, there are similarities in human behaviour such as facial expression from which we can hypothesise meaning (although there is now some contention about whether facial expression does have universal meaning[8]) but remember that all human beings are unique. The meaning behind their signals will have a specific slant within the context of their own internal and external worlds. As guesswork can easily lead us in the wrong direction, we must proceed with caution for any interpretation. If, given this, you are wondering why bother gathering data at all, recall that the purpose of being a human being detective is not for the manager to find the right answer, as in a 'whodunnit' novel, but to help the individual to find it themselves. The process of facilitating another to understand more of the *what*, *how* and *why* of their behaviour through your genuine interest, support, listening and tentative hypotheses is more likely to create sustained change in them than a ready-made solution you spent hours considering on your own.

There now, you are off the hook. It's not a manager's job to 'fix' other human beings. Not at all. You may become an expert data-gatherer but you can never be an expert in interpretation. The only person who can truly interpret this data is the individual himself. By accepting our role as a human being detective, however, we are acknowledging that there is more to each and every one of us than the metaphorical 'duck' we see floating on the water; those psychological 'feet' are paddling away and setting the direction for everything on view. By seeking to understand all the layers of our full human selves, we can release potential, improve motivation, increase contentment and, most likely, boost productivity because we increase the likelihood of resolving detrimental human being issues.

What next?

Your skills as a detective have the potential to yield information about each layer of our human being self. To clarify what to look for, a short excursion into the nature of each layer follows, starting with the most obvious one – behaviour (the *what*).

CHAPTER 4

Why Look at Behaviour, the *What*?

B ehaviour is the result of our genes, our learning, our motivation and our thoughts, whether conscious or otherwise. It's our voices using language and it's our hands pulling a lever on a machine, holding scissors to cut hair, stirring a saucepan to bring food to the restaurant table, painting a canvas or the Forth Bridge, moving a computer mouse to design a car or a building or a spreadsheet or a speech, or any one of millions of other actions. Behaviour is how we move about in the world. Being alive is about behaviour.

What's *what* got to do with work?

This is a no-brainer. Behaviour is what an organisation wants. It's what leads to output. It's what we get paid for. Diving into an Olympic pool from the top board with a backwards flip and a triple somersault is behaviour. Winning the diving competition is output. If there's no behaviour, nothing happens.

Behavioural theories of management and leadership do not focus on innate traits or capabilities. Instead, they look at what employees, managers and leaders actually do, identifying the specific behaviours required to deliver the desired output. This emphasis on observable actions allows behaviour to be classified, measured, shaped and tutored and, because we can see behaviour, it's reasonably straightforward to know when it happens. By sticking to objective measures, assessors and managers are encouraged to direct and evaluate performance in a consistent way that displaces the old school tie, nepotism and favouritism because, unless an individual can be seen to deliver specific behaviours, or is deemed capable of learning them, he will not meet the criteria for a role. This overcomes the effect of charm and other characteristics that can exaggerate ability because these become irrelevant if the target behaviour is not displayed. Further, the very process of identifying the behaviours required for a role often helps improve performance because it forces an organisation to ask the question: what must happen for the desired output to be achieved? Given these advantages, it is little wonder that looking at behaviour has become the standard method for managing performance.

Cautions when applying a behavioural approach

If only it were that simple. As you would expect, for something as complicated as assessing and managing behaviour, there are many pitfalls along the way. Studying behaviour in laboratory conditions is an exact procedure where precise definitions, detailed observation and thorough recording allow for an accurate account of human actions. In the real world, conditions are not so rarefied and our ability to direct and assess behaviour with such precision isn't possible.

Behaviour doesn't occur in a vacuum: Our behaviour is not a free-floating activity. It takes place within the context of the system in which we live or work. When one of my children shouts '*it's not my fault, he hit me first*', I may see his point but I also have to remember who hit whom on the last occasion, the history behind why my otherwise delightful sons have fallen out and my own history of reactions to events of this kind. To be honest, in the moment I am likely to answer '*I don't care. Just stop hitting each other*' but this only puts the problem on hold. To get to grips with their repeated arguments, I need to understand the basis of their relationship with each other and with me. I need to consider what purpose this behaviour serves.

If we see one act in isolation from its context, we risk missing its point. At minimum, we need to be aware of the other variables that form a web around an action because, if we want to produce change, we might have to pull, push or snap one or more strands of it in the process. In a work web (or *system*) this is tricky and often involves variables outside of our immediate control – Mr Jones from Finance who doesn't want to play ball, Mrs Smith in Procurement who is more concerned about meeting her savings target than getting you the resource you need, and the entire IT department who have decided to install new software at the very time you need to run a program.

Thinking from a systems perspective is not something that we are taught in school other than in the science curriculum. Consequently, it doesn't come naturally to many managers when applied to organisations and to people. Systems thinking requires us to look wider, deeper and longer-term than the simple task and individual behaviour that lies before us. Alas, when pressure is placed on producing immediate results, the additional complexity posed by a systems perspective means that it's often the first casualty. To be of value, behavioural approaches have to take a systemic perspective. Looking at my behaviour without appreciating how the environment impacts upon me will tell you little about what I am capable of doing (or not doing). By focusing on isolated behaviours, managers risk over- or underestimating the contribution made by individuals, teams or departments.

Who likes a straightjacket? The introduction of scientific management by the engineer Frederick Taylor[9] in the early part of the last century revolutionised how people were organised and managed. He suggested that optimum performance could be achieved by identifying and standardising the behaviour required to complete a job, thereby reducing the scope for human error and the human tendency to stray away from the task in hand. There is no doubt that scientific management had a significant impact on productivity in manufacturing but by choosing to jettison the human element it failed to recognise that human beings are not too keen on the straightjacket it imposes. People like a degree of autonomy. People bring different views, different ways of doing things. People interfere with the science of scientific management.

Most of us welcome guidelines to help direct our work because they provide a gauge against which the extent of our achievement and success can be shown. However, when guidelines turn into directives in which behaviours are prescribed in detail, they are likely to be less well received. Hence, it is not surprising to find that in call centres, where the shadow of scientific management still lurks, staff attrition rates within the first six months of employment can reach as high as 50%.[10] People don't like being treated as machines. Using a computer system to monitor specific human behaviour (like the time it takes an employee to go to the toilet) suggests an absence of trust and trust is a human being essential. Some behavioural approaches can take behaviour management a step too far.

We all see behaviour in the same way, don't we? In my house, we have a set of pasta bowls that I insist are green but my husband, children and father insist are blue. My sense of colour is definitely not the same as theirs. Interestingly, my sister agrees with me. She's a green person. At this basic level, members of my family see the world differently. In a similar way, human beings don't 'see' behaviour in an identical manner because, as noted previously, we add a personal filter to whatever is before us. We can't help it. Try asking two people to describe what they heard at a meeting they both attended and you will most likely find significant discrepancies between their accounts. What's more, our emotional response to the same behaviour can vary between people and with time; what we balk at one day we may pass over the next. It seems that both our perception and our interpretation of what we have 'seen' are selective.

Behaviour today versus behaviour tomorrow: Senior management teams are charged with creating a vision for the future and a strategy to achieve it but, as the recent financial downturn has shown, predicting the future is a challenging task. Visions and strategies have to be adjusted as the environment twists and turns in surprising ways, meaning that what's right today may be out of fashion or directly unhelpful tomorrow. In this unpredictable world, managers at the next level down, who have the job of translating strategy into behaviours for their people, face an equally difficult task. How can they provide specific guidance when the demands from their leaders shift? With one set of economic conditions, bank employees may be encouraged to lend, lend, lend. In another, they may be required to do the very opposite. As political and social agendas shift, social workers may be asked to broaden the criteria for the removal of children into care. As policies change again, they may require children to be kept with their natural parents for longer. In summary, while behavioural templates work reasonably well in a stable environment, they risk becoming quickly out of date in a rapidly changing world.

The behavioural approach is robust, isn't it? There's one major problem with behaviour. There's so much of the darned stuff. It comes at us from all angles and, much of the time, there's more going on than one, two or a whole team of people can register. If you've ever had to observe and count specific behaviours, live or from a recording, you'll know how difficult, time-consuming and boring it is to categorise every action. To make this task practical, we rely instead on a representative sample of behaviour as an indicator of the behaviour overall. That's what we do when reviewing performance at appraisal; examples of behaviour are used rather than listing every occurrence. To simplify matters further, we often give these samples a numeric or alphanumeric rating to represent their quality and/or quantity. Unfortunately, once we start to treat behaviour in this way, we introduce the potential for distortion.

A typical problem is that our sample of behaviour is not representative of the individual's behaviour at other times (e.g. does the well-rehearsed presentation at an interview tell us much about how an individual conveys his views on a day-to-day basis?). Our sample may be contaminated by other events happening in the environment (e.g. observing a receptionist at a hotel on a day that the computer system is down will affect the behaviour seen) or changes within the individual (e.g. when I have a heavy cold, I am not as communicative as when I am physically well). Proving that a sample is representative takes time and resources and the research needed to do so is rarely undertaken in a work situation. Mostly, managers have to rely on feeling comfortable that the sample they are using is based on their wider experience of an individual's behaviour.

The problem with ratings: Once intricate behaviour is summarised into a single rating other problems arise. A rating is a way of creating a shorthand code. However, with something as complex as human behaviour, unless we have thousands of ratings to account for thousands of actions (which would make the rating system pointless), any rating inevitably draws a ring around a wide range of behaviours. For example, if the rating given for a set of behaviours is at the mid-point of a norm group (say a 3 on a scale of 1 to 5), does that mean my behaviour is at the mid-point in every respect? Or does it indicate behaviour at a level of 4 in most regards but at a particularly poor level 1 in another respect, making it difficult to award the 4 overall? Then again, it might represent a mixture of all ratings leading to an average score of 3. As a consequence, depending on how the rating scale is used, ratings given for different people may be the same but the behaviour that underlies them may vary considerably. When we try to concertina complex behaviour to fit into the same shaped rating box, there is bound to be a problem with the fit.

What's more, when we are given numbers to play with, there is a natural desire to manipulate them. Human beings like statistics and the inferences we can draw from them. But if our sophisticated analysis does not compare like with like, the old saying of 'garbage in leading to garbage out' will hold. To compound matters, if the output of such manipulation is presented as a beautifully produced report with coloured bar charts and rows of figures, it's easy to be convinced that the numbers tell the truth. But which truth? The scope for errors in this kind of analysis is significant and that's before a manager makes a personal interpretation of the data through his own unique set of filters. In summary, without appropriate design and scrutiny, it's possible to create behavioural approaches that have an appearance of science but which the data does not justify.

The burgeoning assessment industry is busy dealing with cautions of this nature to bring greater rigour into behavioural assessment. Organisations, too, are becoming more savvy in their scrutiny of behavioural tools. However, the truth of the matter is that the day-to-day use of behavioural methods still lies with managers who may or may not appreciate the intricacies of creating valid data.

Behaviour and sustainable change

What if we have identified the precise behaviour we want for the current context, have kept an eye on likely future demands and have tied down our assessment processes to a high degree of accuracy – is that enough to ensure success? Maybe yes but quite possibly no. Simply telling someone how to behave does not ensure that they will follow orders. If we make people act in a certain way through coercion (do this or be penalised), we must be ready to watch the seeds of discontent grow into bigger and thornier problems. If we truly want people to use their potential and develop in a way that benefits an organisation in the long term, we must harness their motivation for this task. Certainly, identifying the *what* (i.e., if deemed to be performing well, what would an observer see a person do, and what would be the result of this behaviour) is a critical first stage in this journey and, in my experience, is a stage often overlooked. However, on its own, understanding *what* does not take us far enough to result in deeply rooted change. Without getting beneath *what* to discover *how* and *why*, individuals may deliver what is needed today but not necessarily do so tomorrow.

Where does that leave us with behaviour?

These difficulties certainly don't mean that we should discard the behavioural approach. They are small problems when compared with the benefits that a detailed examination of behaviour can provide. People need to know what is expected of them and a behavioural description is the best way of providing this. Yet studying behaviour gives us more than this. It gives us clues about the layers beneath, the layers that may have a significant impact on the long-term use of potential. A good human being detective never stops looking at behaviour (including language as a behaviour), using clues in the here and now to help shape future performance. However, appreciating the limitations of a purely behavioural approach is the key to gathering and using this data reliably. Here are a few pointers to help you on your way.

Start with output. What's all this behaviour for? It's quite easy to fill a day with frenetic activity without really understanding what this busy behaviour aims to achieve. It should be possible to relate all tasks, and then all behaviours, to a meaningful goal. To do so, make sure you can complete the following for yourself and for your team members: *I will have succeeded when X and Y and Z occur* (where X, Y and Z are end points, not parts of a process). Then work backwards to tasks and behaviours needed to make this output possible. If the end goal is vague or missing, you will be fortunate indeed not to waste considerable time, resources and goodwill.

Allow flexibility in the behaviour you expect from team members in order to accommodate individual differences. There are many ways to the same end. Because that's the way it's always been done (or you would do it) does not mean it's the way it must be done now.

Demand robust design, evaluation and monitoring of behavioural methodologies. Don't accept them at face value. Try not to be swayed by slick graphics and marketing hype. Generally, the fancier the packaging, the more cautious you need to be.

Consider carefully the individual behavioural categories against which people are assessed. Check if they are suitable for your people with the roles and tasks they perform. Do not be afraid to edit behavioural frameworks (or ask for help to do so) if it's a stretch to make them applicable for your team members. A badly fitting shoe is not only useless for walking but causes pain.

Don't accept behavioural information without establishing how it was collected. Ratings without context are meaningless.

Get beneath numerical analysis to ensure it's meaningful and not a spurious average of averages. Be willing to look for the individual human beings within the data – what does it tell you about them at a deeper level, the *how* and the *why*?

Give greater thought to the wider system in which human beings operate. Be cleverer at looking at interactions and better at drawing complicated systems on white boards (well, thinking about systems, anyway). Be willing to examine your own part in the system that is your team. Consider which parts of the broader environment need to be tweaked or given a major shake up to allow your team members to give of their best.

What next?

Observing, recording and interpreting behaviour is a time-intensive affair. Fortunately, we don't have to start from a blank sheet of paper. Tools that aim to capture repeated patterns of behaviour, in terms of recurring styles or preferences, give us a head start for both understanding and predicting *how* an individual is likely to behave. So, it's to the *how* that we turn next.

CHAPTER 5

Why Look at Style and Preferences, the *How*?

H uman beings are born with a different approach to *how*. We don't arrive as an empty sheet. We may have a tabula rasa as far as our thoughts are concerned but our processing systems are far from blank. Our personalised genetic template means that we arrive ready equipped with a temperament that influences our emotionality, sociability, attention, persistence, reactivity and so forth. If you have children, you may have been aware, as I was, of just how different they are from the moment they take their first breath. Studies of identical and non-identical twins have shown that our genes play a significant part in determining the temperament with which we begin our journey in life.[11] From this starting point, experiences carve their effect on us, creating the complex personalities we then become but with our temperamental differences running alongside. We approach the world from our own standpoint from the very beginning. We have a preferred style of *how* from the off.

What's *how* got to do with work?

In complex jobs, where the behaviour required cannot be defined or predicted easily, employees have greater freedom about how they play their part in meeting an organisation's goals. Naturally, this freedom is not a free-for-all. If I achieve my goals brilliantly but, in the process, create mayhem and discord around me, the collateral damage done may be too high a price to pay for my achievement. *How* we go about our work matters. From an accountant's perspective, the cost/benefit ratio must be firmly in favour of benefit. Organisations are often poor at recognising, and particularly poor at evaluating, collateral damage where a favourable end can be used to justify, or at least gloss over, a dodgy means (the *how*). For instance, while the profits kept rolling in from the mis-selling of PPI policies, several banks seemed not to notice how these profits were being derived until they were caught out. Or consider the department where fifteen people resigned in one year after the arrival of a new boss. It was not until the sixteenth resignation that the senior team recognised the detrimental impact the new individual was having on their business. In their eyes, the leader was performing. The cost to their business in terms of staff turnover, lost revenue and reputation was evidence that the collateral cost of this 'performance' was too high. Both the *what* and the *how* matter.

Recognising that more is required to manage performance than setting objectives and prescribing behaviours (the *what*), organisations have sought to find ways to examine the *how*. Two approaches have stolen centre stage in this regard: competency frameworks and psychometric instruments.

The ups and downs of competency frameworks

Competency frameworks[12] define the boundaries between acceptable and unacceptable behaviour by providing a common language through which the *how* can be described. Instead of having to agree a unique set of behaviours required for every circumstance, a comprehensive list of competencies provides a ready-made list of ways of working, from personal to technical, which should cover most situations. With an overarching definition, each competency is usually further described by a (not exhaustive) set of example behaviours which give the flavour of what is expected whenever a situation demands this competency. As competencies are said to reside within the individual, they are often used as predictors of future performance. If I am viewed to have strength in one competency, then that strength should be displayed in the future as much as it is now. It's not surprising, therefore, to find that competency frameworks have become the core structure around which recruitment, promotion and development processes are frequently built.

The upsurge of interest in frameworks of this kind has put *how* firmly on the agenda. It has forced managers to consider and then define what they are looking for in their people and caused them to justify their people decisions beyond personal whim. This is undoubtedly all good stuff. But, like the purely behavioural approach, the competency methodology has its limitations and, if not addressed, these issues can make us trundle off in the wrong direction, rather like following a signpost twisted out of line. Be warned.

Language distortion: Drawing up a list of competencies is like trying to distil the essence of a job (or a class of jobs, or a management level), onto a single page. It's difficult to get right. It's part analysis and part art. The analytical bit involves taking copious behavioural examples, derived from detailed interviews and direct observation, and then sorting them into general categories that are distinct from each other. This might be achieved the old-fashioned way with a pile of cards and a large table to lay out patterns of behaviour or it might be achieved through some whizzy software. Whichever method is used, the art bit has to come next – choosing a label for each category. You may think that the label given to a competency isn't particularly important as long as the examples given clarify its meaning but unfortunately it matters very much. The words used as a label become the shorthand by which a competency is known and words don't travel alone. They have associations from other parts of our lives as their companions. These interfering references to past and present experiences can easily overshadow the true meaning that was determined from the analysis. If the label doesn't feel right, or a word is used colloquially in a different way, human beings will distort the meaning, often going with their own interpretation of the label rather than the behavioural 'anchors' that describe it. A competency analysis may be first class but what human beings then do with it is another matter.

The desire for a tick in every box: When assessing against a list of prescribed competencies, there is an almost-hypnotic urge to require individuals to be good at the whole lot, to hit 10/10 on each competency. To lag behind in one area is to have a performance shortfall and a 'development need'.

Now this doesn't make logical sense because in most frameworks it isn't possible to be equal on all fronts. Strength in some areas can lessen performance in another. It's like sitting on one end of a see-saw. If you have enough weight in one area to pull the see-saw down, the other end will be lighter. In assessment centres, it's rare to find someone who performs equally well across all areas. When they do, it's often because the tasks on which they are being assessed are too easy for them. Give them a more stretching task and the performance on different competencies often becomes differentiated. Human beings differ in the way they think and feel. Our brains do not function in exactly the same way, which means that individual people have individual profiles. If I am particularly strong at listening, giving time to my staff and clients, getting to the bottom of client matters, I may not be as speedy on delivering other tasks. Another person may be a whizz at cracking through all the tasks on his list but not give time to listen to staff and clients' views along the way. Which is right and which is wrong? As you guessed, it depends on the role and the demands of the organisation at that time.

Templates can be blunt instruments: The tendency to use generic frameworks to cover wide categories of roles (i.e. all management grades, all leadership roles) means that a fair amount of bodging must be done to make the system applicable to all. In addition, because creating competency frameworks is a costly and time-consuming business, they tend to be updated only occasionally yet risk going out of date fairly quickly. An organisation must respond to the changing dynamics of its market and, as a result, the demands placed on its staff shift.

This has to be reflected in its competency framework otherwise the paperwork can drive performance in the wrong direction.

Consistency is not always desirable: By recruiting and developing against a single template, an organisation exposes itself to risk. The wise organisation recognises that it can't have all things from all men and women all the time. It allows for a variety of profiles, a mix of people, bringing a range of possible approaches to *how* they work. It wants difference so that it can be agile in times of change. It does not turn down great strength in one area just because one or two other competency areas are lacking. It accepts difference because, if well managed, differences are not a problem. Good managers look for ways to work with difference, to fit human beings to roles, drawing on their strengths, rather than expect a bland level of conformity across all competencies. A positive example of this is the way innovative IT organisations are actively recruiting people on the autistic spectrum for their great strengths in technology and coding.[13] The areas with which people on the spectrum struggle are outweighed by the talents they bring. What a splendid reminder that human beings do not come competency list-shaped.

Reality or wishful thinking: The underlying premise of competency analysis is that it identifies characteristics and skills carried by individuals across situations. Therefore, when using a competency framework for assessment we should be able to identify a population of people who share similar attributes and who are likely to behave consistently (the *how*) in different circumstances. If only it were this straightforward. Many years ago, I was involved in a study analysing data from a partner selection assessment centre. The results showed that ratings for an individual's performance were correlated more highly within each exercise than across them, i.e. the situation had more influence on performance than underlying characteristics of the individual.[14] This 'exercise effect' has been found many times since. In assessment centres at least, competencies are not fixed characteristics. Individuals don't have a consistent *how*.

If competencies aren't stable, then what is being assessed? Perhaps such frameworks are simply our best guess at what ought to be constant, allowing for a wide (sometimes very wide) margin of variation. But, if they represent only our aspiration for performance, we must be very cautious in how we use data derived from them unless we have concrete statistical proof that they are valid predictors of future performance. However neat and well researched our competency framework, we cannot assume that individuals will always behave in a specific way regardless of the situation; that's not how human beings are made. *How* is not fixed and can vary considerably depending on the surrounding circumstances.

The ins and outs of psychometric tools

In addition to competency frameworks, organisations are increasingly employing psychometric tools to gain a short-cut understanding of the *how* of work. At an individual level, the information they provide can be an invaluable resource for coaching, development activities and career counselling. By providing a language than explains broader interests and styles, they help look at the 'fit' between an individual and different tasks, roles, cultures and career paths. At a team level, understanding preferences and styles can be used to diffuse conflict by explaining the range of ways people approach the same task, making team members more tolerant and accepting of difference. Although used less often at a larger group level, psychometric instruments can also be used to determine the overall profile of a department, or even a whole organisation.

In the right hands, such tools undoubtedly support our understanding of human beings, allowing us to make greater sense of behaviour. You will have guessed by now, however, that a list of cautions is to follow because, when misused, those inviting paper- or computer-delivered inventories and tests can be misleading or, at worst, quite dangerous. Hence, a few warnings are due.

Selection bias: When I assessed the entire marketing department of a large consultancy, around forty people in total, all but one was found to have a creative, abstract preference in the way they solved problems. They liked each other, they understood each other and they tended to work in the same way but, alas, they were all heading off the edge of a cliff together because they neglected the things that they didn't like. In this case, it was the more detailed administration needed to keep the department functioning. 'Who does the admin?' I asked. 'Me,' cried a lone voice, mournfully, 'because no one else will.' The depressed speaker was, of course, the one individual with the opposite style.

Such organisational bias towards one approach can be due to career preferences – if people with this style are more attracted to marketing, and perhaps more successful at it, recruiters will have a skewed pool from which to choose. If this preference is also used as a psychometric template for selection, the bias will be strengthened. If, as is likely, the selector has this style himself, the bias will be blooming like yeast in warm dough. Human beings like to select in their own likeness with the result that selectors keep choosing the same type of candidate over and over again. Maybe that's what they want but the risk from this lack of variation is the same as when selecting repeatedly on identical competency profiles. Organisations need a range of styles and preferences to thrive. Limiting this range makes it difficult to change course when the environment requires it. If used inappropriately, psychometric instruments can foster this bias. Of course, if used wisely, the very same tools can foster a more balanced population. It's how the data is used that counts.

Profile-ist cultures: While we're talking about bias, another issue to watch for is the ease with which organisations can become 'profile-ist' where certain styles and preferences, once acknowledged, are deemed superior to others. The widely used Myers–Briggs Type Indicator is a case in point. In analytical, commercial environments, some preferences are often, mistakenly, regarded as unbusinesslike and can be undervalued, along with the people who hold them.[15] With aptitude tests, it is also quite easy to slip into an intellectual elitism where scoring above or below a fixed-point marks an individual as 'clever' or 'not clever enough' regardless of their real-life performance. I recall an individual who held a senior role in a bank but whose score on an aptitude test was extremely low, so low that I reassessed him with another measure but with the same result. On further investigation, there was an explanation. This individual had grown up in a deprived area and received a very poor quality of education when young. Despite this, he got to university where he did well, had a successful career and was now flourishing in a challenging role. There may be issues is his ability to apply his thinking beyond his own area of expertise but, in his field, he is recognised as a star. If today's ubiquitous online screening processes had been in place when he was first recruited, he would not have cleared the first hurdle and his talent would have been lost to the organisation. It will be interesting to discover whether recent changes in selection processes, where entry based on academic attainment (and its relationship to social class) have been replaced by in-house measures of aptitude and 'strengths',[16] do indeed lead to a fairer and more effective system or simply substitute old ways with a different type of elitism and discrimination.

Not all measures are valid: I know that the handbook that accompanies a psychometric instrument doesn't rate highly on the best holiday reading list but, to have confidence in an instrument, it's essential to know how it was constructed and how its internal validity was tested. To find this out, you have to get elbow-deep into the manual, beyond the 'how to administer' section, right into the numbers. If there are no statistics on test construction, don't even think about using the instrument. It could have been drawn up on the back of an envelope after several bottles of wine by someone with a pet theory but little experience. Even without the wine, it wouldn't be valid unless there is research to prove the theory on which it is based and show that the measure does what it says it does. Just because an instrument is popular and people like it, doesn't mean it's valid (hint: there are a few widely used tools that fall into this bracket).

All instruments can't be used for all people: So, if the data is all present and correct, does it make the instrument robust? Well, that depends on how we want to use it. To be valid, we must use the instrument according to the parameters on which it was developed. Is the norm group used for comparison relevant to our people? A measure designed for graduates may be inappropriate for senior managers; a personality measure designed for a North American population may not be suitable for use in other parts of the world (unless it has been specifically adjusted to account for this); can it be used with people who will be completing it in their second language? Were the norms created or revised recently? What was accurate in 1990 may not be accurate today. Such questions mean that it's trickier to find an appropriate psychometric instrument to meet your needs than you may have realised. Study the manual, take your time and get specialist help if you are unsure.

Aptitude tests and inventories of style or preference are not absolute: Sorry, but we're not done with the validity issue yet. Psychometric tests and inventories show aptitude or preference not certainty. Unless the research has been done to show that a particular score on an instrument correlates with performance in a role, it cannot be regarded as a valid predictor of performance in that job, i.e. how the aptitude or preference will be lived out in practice. Also, when an organisation does have the evidence to suggest an instrument predicts performance, it cannot be assumed that what predicts today's high performance will also predict that of tomorrow – the world and its demands change. On this basis, using psychometric tools as a single assessment method is of dubious merit. Using them as an in/out initial screening tool, a common practice for graduate recruitment, is also worrying. While this may increase the accuracy of selection on some fronts (e.g. increase the number of employees who pass their accountancy exams at first attempt), it risks creating a uniform pot of employees who may be less able to deal with the unforeseen problems that the environment may throw up in the next decade or two. In general, psychometric instruments are most useful when used to help explain a performance after the assessment has been concluded, as means into further discussion, or for development, not as a single deciding criterion.

The handy excuse: From an individual's point of view, the results of a psychometric instrument can provide a handy excuse for staying the same – 'well, that's just how I am' or 'I would if I could but it's no good asking me to do that. It's not my style.' Human beings are not fixed entities. We grow. Yes, we have preferences that lead our focus to fall one way rather than another but experience shapes us too. Growing as a person is about expanding our horizons rather than restricting them, seeing the world from different perspectives and choosing which one we want to follow. We can change but, as Jung describes so beautifully,[17] with age we human beings can also become entrenched, fixed in our views, our principles and our way of living. It's important to remember this when giving or receiving feedback from psychometric measures. The information they provide concerns *how* an individual may operate now, not *who* they are. The *how* and the *who* can keep developing if we, and others around us, allow it.

Where does that leave us with style and preference?

Like pieces of a jigsaw puzzle, I'm most likely to feel comfortable when my preferred style and my aptitudes fit closely with the demands of my role. I'll probably be best placed to deliver a good performance too. Therefore, techniques that yield data on style and preference, and make this match more likely, are valuable managerial tools. But to derive this value, competency-based approaches and psychometric instruments must be used in a carefully controlled way. Unfortunately, organisations have been increasingly seduced by slick marketing, and the promise of an easier life, without always taking heed of this need for caution. According to Moss (2015),[18] a survey by *Personnel Today* and Network HR found that, while more than three-quarters of respondents considered psychometric tests to be a powerful tool for recruitment, 30% reported it was not a requirement for their staff to be trained in these tests before using them with candidates. If I were a candidate applying to one of these organisations, I would be concerned. Actually, I'd be annoyed.

At an organisational level, getting selection and development decisions wrong has consequences in terms of long-term performance and profitability. At an individual level, the consequences are more personal. Human beings are on the receiving end of such misjudgement. Human beings get turned down based on the outcome of a single, computer-administered test. Human beings are told they have weaknesses to address while their strength, and potential value to an organisation, is overlooked. Human beings are told they must be everything on a checklist of attributes, that they must fit the mould, when the mould itself may be faulty.

What is a manager to do? Managers need data on *how*. Fortunately, there is no need to discard the value that competency frameworks and psychometric measures provide because, in most cases, it's not the measures of *how* that are at fault but the way we apply them. If we improve our knowledge and understanding of how to use these measures appropriately, then we can have greater confidence in them and obtain a higher reward for the investment in time and cash they require. So here come the reminders.

In general:

- **Be willing to spend time helping your people to understand how they work** because getting to grips with *how* is vital for their development. It helps individuals appreciate the unique approach they bring to their work, what kind of work life will be most satisfying for them and it sheds light on problem areas. Clarifying *how* makes it more likely that you will see more of the behaviour you want in order to achieve the output the organisation needs.

- **The easiest way to get information on *how* is simply to discuss it with the individual concerned.** Because other methods exist doesn't mean you have to use them. You don't need to be a psychologist to do this.

Use the data that's before your eyes – what you see the person do on a day-to-day basis. What trends do you see?

- **If you do collect more structured data, be very clear with those involved about the purpose of this process** and how the information derived will be used. Take all confidentiality issues regarding personal data seriously. Expect legal cases if you don't. Make sure, too, that you don't waste data. If you collect it for recruitment or assessment, use it also for development.

- **Give feedback on any data you collect** but allow the individual to lead on its interpretation. You can question or challenge this interpretation but the individual's perspective is invaluable.

- **When looking at *how* in a team context, be sure to agree explicit ground rules** for sharing personal information about style and preference before any disclosure is made. Do not tolerate any style elitism.

- **Do not assume that any profile of *how* that emerges is set in stone.** We all change.

Competency data:

- **Ensure that the competencies you use fit the specific role and level of the individual concerned rather than highly general, supposedly fit-for-all lists.** Competency analysis is not an exact science. It produces a language to guide and/or evaluate approximate categories of behaviour. The process of shoehorning all relevant behaviour into a single list will undoubtedly lead to a degree of fudging which can mask significant variations in behaviour.

- **When assessing people about *how*, it is particularly important to capture situational differences** even if the assessment system doesn't have a box to record them. Otherwise, we lose valuable information and can be left with a bland overview that means little. From a systems perspective, many variables beyond our style and aptitude influence the way we behave which is why *how* is not always demonstrated in a consistent way. For example, an individual's interpersonal skills may be exceptional in a work situation but only average at a cocktail party made up of strangers.

- **Remember that a human being is more than a set of checklists.** Having broken a performance apart into its constituent competencies or parts of a psychological profile, don't forget to put them back together to take a holistic view. How competencies and profiles fit together and interact, how one skill or preference compensates for another, is far more interesting and relevant than each area of performance considered on its own.

Psychometric instruments:

- **Human beings are not one-dimensional creatures so do not expect to gain a full picture of a person from a single instrument of style, preference or aptitude.** Always look at psychometric data alongside other sources of information such as observed behaviour, information about past experience, job trials etc.

- **Test the robustness of the tools you use.** Never mind what HR says, do your own research. Ask for the handbook. Check how a measure was constructed. Check the norm group. Is it valid for your people, for your purpose? Don't presume that the statistics on validity and reliability are beyond your reach. They may be dull but they're really not that complicated.

- **Ensure that the people administering and interpreting instruments have the correct training** to do so and are following the required protocols.

- **For selection, clarify that relevant research has been carried out to give you confidence that each instrument used does accurately predict later performance** in the role. Ensure that this research is ongoing and not a one-off. If there is no research, you are basing your decisions on guesswork.

- **Check how easy it is for applicants to fake data.** If a candidate thinks you want outgoing people, he may well have a good go at pretending to be the life and soul of the party in a questionnaire, at interview or elsewhere. The resulting profile will be nonsense.

- **When using aptitude tests, if you want meaningful data, allow everyone to practise thoroughly in advance** so that the real test is done on an equal basis. With aptitude tests, there can be a strong practice effect (i.e. performance improves with repeat attempts at similar tests). 'Thoroughly' means more than one or two questions. It means having a full version of an equivalent test to try.

- **From time to time, take an overview of the data available for your team or department or indeed organisation.** Look for selection bias. Are you all the same? What is the potential impact of favouring one style? What happens to the people who do it differently? Who tends to leave and who tends to stay? If you need more variety, how could that be addressed? Are you making best use of the range of styles and aptitudes you have available?

What next?

In our simplified model of human beings, style, aptitude and preference sit one level below surface behaviour. They help explain *how*. To get to grips with *why*, we need to look at a deeper level, at where our values and beliefs reside.

CHAPTER 6

Why Look at Values and Beliefs, the *Why*?

Wouldn't it be fascinating if we could remember what we thought about as a baby, to go back to a point when our understanding of the world was at its near beginning? Researchers have discovered that, although babies appear helpless, they are in fact active learners, building their understanding of their environment from their earliest experiences onwards.[19] In the first few years of life, our brains are positively alight with new learning, turning experience into a thinking structure that will be built upon, adapted and then used to support us through the years to come. This cognitive structure takes the form of thoughts and feelings, which, with time, are crafted into a set of beliefs about how the world works. As mentioned in an earlier chapter, our childhood experiences are particularly potent in the formation of this framework because they come first. They are the initial building blocks of our thoughts and their arrangement affects where subsequent blocks are positioned.

Such early beliefs are so much a part of us that they become automatic. Indeed, they may feel as though they are the only beliefs possible; they are just the way the world is. It's not unusual for children to assume that everyone thinks the way they do. It's not unusual for many adults to think that too. Yet, in this as in all things, although we can share similar beliefs with our fellow human beings, the overall structure of our thinking is unique to each individual. Even siblings brought up in the same household, and who have much in common, will differ in how they approach and react to the world. Each will have created their own slant on their shared experiences.

Are values and beliefs the same thing? I'm not sure that our use of language is precise enough to make an exact distinction but, to me, beliefs are views on how the world operates and values are our aspirations of how it *should* operate. Beliefs centre on what is. Values centre on what might be – what we aspire to have, to achieve or to become, along with our desires about the type of society we want to exist even if there is little chance of this occurring. Beliefs and values are formed in a similar way. They are the seat of both hope and disappointment for, even though I believe something to be true, I can still wish that is was not.

Our beliefs and values create the filters used to determine the personal relevance of incoming information. They are central to our emotional processing, our 'heart', as they have the ability to trigger or calm an emotional reaction. They alter how we behave, how we think. They act as our own personal guide, a set of brakes or a sensitive accelerator.

I think I know what I believe, but I'm not so sure...

Some of our beliefs are well-known companions. Indeed, a number may be so prominent in our thinking that they cast a long shadow over others, pushing conflicting thoughts into a dark recess. Other beliefs have a hazy form or are not in our conscious awareness at all, requiring determined excavation to bring to the surface. We experience the consequences of hidden beliefs when our emotions react to a situation but we can't put our finger on why.

A belief that made sense in the past may not do so now

I remember very little of my childhood years before the age of four and only fragments from several years afterwards. Therefore, I can't recall the experiences that may have shaped my early thoughts on how the world worked. To make sense of what formed my beliefs, I have instead to draw on any evidence I can gather about my past (from memories of my parents, siblings or friends, from photographs and mementoes). Or, in the absence of evidence, I just have to guess. There's a small snag here. Young children do not behave like Sherlock Holmes. They do not gather and interpret information in a cold and dispassionate way. Instead, when we are young, events that have a strong emotional significance when they occur are given particular emphasis in the belief creation process. For instance, the one occasion on which a grandmother shouted at her grandchild because he broke her best teapot can colour his whole view of her as a frightening person. In comparison, memories of the many, many times she was warm and kind to him may have faded to insignificance. So, when we try to understand the origin of beliefs, we must remember that the information we used as young children to create them may have been partial (e.g. cleaning my plate at mealtimes made my mother happy. I must always eat all the food I am given) or downright faulty (e.g. my parents said I was naughty the day before my dad left home. Therefore, it was my fault they broke up – because I was naughty). As a result, when we examine the logic of our beliefs from today's perspective, the basis for some of them (often the unhelpful beliefs) can be extremely shaky.

The same belief can be helpful and unhelpful

The German psychoanalyst Karen Horney coined the term 'tyranny of the shoulds'.[20] Most people have 'shoulds': beliefs about how we must behave in the world if something bad is not to happen – we 'should' be good or clever or beautiful or brave or quiet or successful or anything at all. Deep-rooted beliefs about how we should behave in the world can be great motivators, providing the energy needed to keep us going against difficulty and pushing us to achieve. Their unquestioned and ready-made nature makes them the automatic choice when looking for reasons to convince ourselves that our motives are sound. So far so good. But Horney's choice of the word 'tyranny' reminds us that ingrained beliefs are not always helpful. There is fear attached to 'should' because, like a nagging parent, it keeps reminding us that unless we fulfil the 'should' we risk falling short as a human being. When 'shoulds' become 'musts', they become a burden and a source of despair, taunting us with the thought that we are not good enough.

Beliefs can change

A wonderful therapist once told me *we cannot change the past but we can our minds*, a phrase that has never left me. When underlying beliefs are unhelpful, identifying, challenging and replacing them with more positive beliefs can make a significant difference to our contentment and well-being. This is the basis of cognitive behaviour therapy but it's also the basis for growing up. Taking responsibility for how we see the world is about taking responsibility for directing our own life. Because we believe something doesn't mean that it's true or that we have to keep believing it. As a child, the environment shaped me. As an adult, I have choice. I can change my mind.

What's *why* got to do with work?

Isn't it rather impertinent to think that a manager has any right to dig into another person's values and beliefs? I couldn't agree with you more. It isn't the manager's business as long as everything is going well. But what about when it's not all hunky dory, when the individual is struggling and may or may not know this, or when his behaviour is impacting on the performance of others? Is it the manager's business then? Quite likely it is because when patterns of behaviour repeat themselves, for good or for not so good, it's values and beliefs that hold them there, going around and around and around in circles.

If you've tried addressing change at the behavioural level, if you've looked at the fit between an individual's style and the role, and neither has helped, you may need to encourage the individual to examine the thinking that underpins the problem – the *why* of beliefs and values. It's up to the individual to decide whether they want to do this or to carry on regardless and accept the consequences; that's their right. But, with enough support and encouragement, they might be willing to challenge some of those unhelpful, automatic beliefs.

But I'm not a therapist!

Absolutely. You're not a therapist and it's extremely important that you remember this. You mustn't meddle in the psychological world of others if you are not both invited and trained to do so. We all need to appreciate our limits. A little knowledge can be a damaging thing and a few days of NLP training or basic coaching skills don't make you a therapist. However, you don't need to be a therapist to help people. After all, people helped each other before the term therapist was invented. Just by being your good human being self, you can be a valuable facilitator of change. By providing an encouraging and supportive environment, you can help people help themselves. The therapist may be interested in where beliefs came from but that's not your business. Your interest is in gently prompting others to uncover the thoughts that may underpin their behaviour. If your intervention serves to clarify the true nature of the problem, a major step forward has been taken.

Where to start when discussing beliefs

How does a people-detective go about discovering values and beliefs without risking a punch on the nose?

Ask the obvious: It's not such a daft idea to ask what you want to know straight out if the situation is right. You don't need clever questions or a sneaky, disguised way of getting at it. Simple, open-ended questions can be enough to get someone thinking and a plain old 'When you do that, what goes through your mind?' can do the trick. Asking shows interest. It implies that we are thinking about the human being before the job, that we care. If we don't ask, we might wait a very long time before the individual raises the issue himself, if ever, and how long have you got? If you're hesitant about having an open conversation, consider why you're not asking. Are you embarrassed or afraid? Perhaps you need to tackle your own values and beliefs before you have this conversation.

Listen so you can hear a pin drop: A missive on listening has already been given about its role as a core skill for human being detectives, but there's school-level listening and there's degree-level listening. When helping people to identify their beliefs, we must be super, super attentive in our listening. That means not being distracted, giving the time needed and genuinely wanting to hear every signal. It also means suspending judgement. You may be flabbergasted by another's beliefs but you should aim not to show that your gast has been flabbered. Human beings make judgements about others all the time. The trick is not to give voice to them because quite often those judgements shift when we have more information to go on.

Tell: Helping people explore what underlies their behaviour should not feel like a one-sided inquisition. Unless your professional role is as a counsellor or therapist, don't make others feel they are being pumped for information. Good communication provides 'give and take' from all parties. I need to hear my manager's perspective (why he wants to help me, how his beliefs can help or hinder him), as much as he needs to hear mine. That's not an excuse for a 'well, if you think you've got problems, just listen to mine...' sort of discussion. Frankly, I'd rather not know the details of my manager's life but a little empathy and a little sharing can make me feel that he's listened to my perspective. 'Tell' does not mean giving the answers either. Giving feedback and explaining expectations can be useful. Telling someone what they should believe won't work because beliefs are ingrained in both our heart and computer. They aren't altered on command.

Don't make a big deal out of it: You've probably had many conversations with people about their beliefs and been told directly or indirectly what matters to them most without realising it. You will have listened to their complaints when the world didn't seem right and their excitement when it was splendid. You may well have spoken to a third party about why one of your people is struggling to change his behaviour. You see, you already inhabit the world of *why*. But if taking the next step of talking directly about beliefs and values makes you feel uncomfortable, you will need to practise some questions about beliefs on yourself first. Without much trouble, you can probably identify the types of questions that wouldn't work on you or, worse, the questions that would irritate you. Then think about the types of questions, and the attitude/behaviour of the questioner, that help you to talk. What is needed to make you open up? If you've got that far, try role playing the conversation in your head – imagine how the conversation might go. If you get the wording clear on a few starting questions, you will find that the other questions will flow.

Pick your moment and know when to stop: If your efforts at help are not well received, desist. Now may just not be the right moment. People rarely tell others something they don't want to disclose even when faced with a highly skilled interviewer. Fortunately, there are clues that help us spot when a road block is approaching. The most obvious is when we're told to mind our own business. Enough said. Strangely, this doesn't happen that often in the manager-subordinate relationship. More likely, you will be treated to distractions that take you off course. It's rather like listening to a politician being interviewed on a radio show when the answers don't seem to match the questions. This doesn't necessarily mean our technique is at fault. If we ask a good question with the right degree of respect and still get nowhere, then we've risked little, lost little and learned something – that the situation is not right for the type of conversation we had in mind. If we carry on regardless, we are likely to be led off at a tangent and it's quite easy to drift on for some time before realising that the conversation has travelled far from its intended purpose. Remember, the moment that, to us, feels right to raise an issue may be the wrong moment for the individual concerned. Meaningful change can only come from the individual and not be imposed upon them. This doesn't mean giving up, however. You can, and probably should, revisit the issue at a later stage.

Get the help you need: You don't have to work on this alone. If you are helping an individual tackle a major problem that requires significant change, you may need to involve other sources of development and support (e.g. coaching, training programmes or counselling) to move things forward. Beliefs are hardy and intransigent blighters so don't expect change to happen overnight. It can take many attempts and considerable determination to chip away at the edifice of belief. Oh, and don't let personal pride become a barrier to asking for help. Some of the human being issues that confront a manager can be highly stressful to deal with. Only a fool refuses a life jacket when he's drowning.

Organisation beliefs and values: culture

In addition to the fundamental beliefs we hold about how the world operates, human beings also carry more specific beliefs about the different environments in which we spend our time. My sons have a clear view of what is ok in school and what isn't. They also know where the blurred lines lie, where they can, and do, test the boundaries. Religious groups, political groups, sports clubs, social groups, indeed all institutions and organisations, must have some degree of shared belief as the 'glue' to hold the membership together. No glue means no broader body and, without it, the organisation risks shattering into as many pieces as there are members. Of course, the glue can be the easy-to-remove type, like on the back of a 'Post-it' note, or the set-rock-solid stuff like superglue. Whatever the type of stickiness, when we speak of the culture of an organisation, that's what we mean.

A work culture creates a mental and emotional blanket, holding people together, as if each member goes about their business wrapped in the fabric of the organisation's personality. Yet, when you're in the midst of it, culture can be a difficult thing to define. It just is, sometimes comforting, sometimes supporting, and sometimes smothering. Mostly, culture doesn't have its feet in facts, resting instead on the shared *perception* of what goes on, on a day-to-day basis, in our place of work. It's what we all believe, even if it isn't accurate. Even if it isn't true. And why do we believe it? Because, as in families, beliefs are acquired in a number of ways – through what we see and hear (evidence, partial or total) and through what gets passed on (from what other people tell us, from what the history of the organisation suggests and from the myths that float in the ether of organisational life). Culture is also no great follower of authority. It prefers to take note of what happens on the ground rather than what is said should happen. A chief executive may give a speech defining the culture he wants but he's highly unlikely to see that culture emerge just because he asks for it. Beliefs don't shift that easily. Indeed, it's possible to fill a library with the number of books that address the topic of culture change and the reason it's a popular topic is because it's so difficult to achieve. However, as culture is not something you can hold in your hand and exists only in the minds of the individuals concerned, coming back to human being basics can give us a few clues about how to understand its influence. Start with yourself, perhaps, and consider three possible scenarios.

What if your beliefs fit nicely with those of the organisation (say, about how people are respected, rewarded and developed or how customers and suppliers are dealt with)? In this instance, you are likely to feel secure in your role and comfortable that you know how to perform. That comfort will free you to focus on what needs to be done. On the downside, you may be so comfortable that you become resistant to innovation or to people that challenge the culture. Then, if the organisation is forced to change because of external factors, the shock that this creates and the ride that follows may be extremely uncomfortable.

What if you are unsure of the fit because the culture of your organisation is unclear or shifts – what's ok one day is not the next? In this instance, the degree of comfort you experience is likely to be affected by the frequency and magnitude of unexpected events. Manageable ripples of change in the daily rules of engagement can be pleasant and invigorating. Frequently occurring, unpredictable or large-scale shifts in the modus operandi lead to anxiety and to mistakes. If you no longer know what is expected, you cannot deliver it. In the absence of clarity, you are most likely to make up your own set of rules and hope to muddle along until matters improve or you find a new job elsewhere. If many people do this, the glue that holds them together eventually fractures. An organisation whose members do not have a common sense of 'who we are' is not destined for success.

What if your beliefs do not fit the prevailing culture (for example, you believe the way customers are sold products is unethical)? Then there will be a cost. You are likely to feel insecure or fearful about what you do on a day-to-day basis and about your future.

If others around you are happy with the way things are, you will have a growing sense that you don't fit in, that you don't belong. And it's highly unlikely that you will perform at your best as your thoughts and emotions will be occupied with this clash of beliefs and values. What, then, are your options? Well, the organisation might kick you out because you are clearly 'not one of us'. Or you might choose to leave it for a different culture where the match is better. Quite likely, though, is that for some time before you go you will simply pretend. Pretend that you go along with the culture. At work, you will say everything is fine but in private (at home, with friends or with trusted colleagues) you will make it clear that everything is certainly not fine. Unfortunately, it's very difficult to keep this pretence going without an outlet to vent your frustration and many home lives are adversely affected as a consequence. Pretending is tiring. It takes energy away from your ability to do a job to the best of your ability. And pretending is rarely viable long-term. If you are brave enough, one day you might try to challenge the ways things are but you will need to be courageous, personally robust, clever and plain lucky to push against an organisation whose members are trundling, or even marching, in the opposite direction.

How to make your team culture human being-friendly

Creating a culture that supports a sustainable organisation is not a one-off activity because culture is about how people think and feel at any one time. It's never a done-deal, especially at a time when the environmental sea in which organisations swim is turbulent and unchartered. Attending to culture is a critical activity for any senior team but it's also the responsibility of each individual manager. That means you can't leave it to someone else to deal with. In your backyard, you need to know the culture that your people follow. Organisations and teams need glue but not superglue; beliefs and values must be wide enough to encompass the majority but not so vague that they can mean just about anything. Here are a few pointers to help you create a culture for real people, not the imaginary, perfect employees of corporate brochures.

- **Recognise the culture that exists**. Any senior team, and any manager, should be alert to the over-reaching beliefs of a workforce or a team. And here I mean real beliefs, the not-so-rosy ones included. The difficult, often hidden, information about culture will only surface if staff feel their views will be respected and acted upon. Even so, you may need an anonymous survey or a disinterested facilitator to get at it.

- **Ask your team to identify 'this is the type of team we want to be'.** These values and beliefs will be an aspiration – how human beings want the organisation to behave. To turn them into reality, you and your team will have to identify specific behaviours that flow from them. What will this culture look like on a grey day in November?

- **Work with the prevailing culture and make change gradually** unless you plan revolution or a radical change in employees (most out, all new in). Your chances of success are greater if you extend, alter or reshape what's there rather than expect people to shift their mindset in a major way. Remember, if you damn the way everything worked in the past, you are, by implication, damning the human beings who spent part of their lives doing what was asked of them. No wonder people become resistant to change. It is possible to make a significant difference in how people perform from a small nudge that leads to a shift in their perspective. An old-fashioned SWOT analysis (strengths, weaknesses, threats and opportunities) is often quite enough to draw out the essentials.

- **Identify the outliers from the existing culture and learn from them rather than reject them.** Encourage challenge and innovation. Draw in rather than throw out and be curious about different beliefs rather than mumble about them behind closed doors. In the end, you may choose not to accept different views but at least you will have done so in a considered way rather than on automatic pilot.

- **Get your team to evaluate how they are doing against their aspirations for culture on a regular basis.** When all's going well, it time for a pat on the back. If it's not, it's time to understand why, not admonishment. Change is all around us and all of us have to change. Helping your people feel that they can cope, and indeed shape change, by exploring their common beliefs and values builds a resilient and more confident team.

Where does this leave us on values and beliefs?

In any interaction, there is always something going on beneath the surface that we can't see or hear. Our brains and emotional systems have an extraordinary work ethic. They don't do time out or lunch or holidays. Whatever's happening outside our body, within it there's a non-stop buzzing of thoughts and feelings based on our values and beliefs as they try to make sense of our environment. This 'something' can be quite minor ('I've heard this before and I feel bored') to a potentially life-threatening reaction (a major emotional shock leading to a rise in blood pressure that leads to thrombosis). Next time you're having a simple chat to your team, remember that there's considerably more going on than meets the eye or ear.

As managers, if we tried to juggle all these variables in our conscious thinking, our metaphorical 'computer' would probably blow out smoke and then shut down in protest. Fortunately for us, most of the time we don't have to work at this level. Much of our everyday interactions take place using straightforward surface behaviour. When I go to the supermarket, I don't need to understand the belief system of the staff helping me. I just need to be able to get my goods, pay for them and leave. In my team, if sufficient time has been spent up front agreeing our direction and how we will work, then the tasks that follow can flow along without much interruption because we have all bought into the plan, meaning that our beliefs (or enough of them) fit with that plan.

BUT as a manager and human being detective, at minimum, you need to be aware that:

- behaviour is driven by beliefs and values;

- your own belief system influences the way you manage others;

- at times, you may need to discuss individual beliefs and values to help human beings who are stuck;

- occasionally, you may need to find the necessary professional support for them and/or you to achieve this;

- at a team and organisation level, you need to be conscious of the health of the shared belief system that binds your people together.

What next?

Although our unique set of beliefs is based on our individual experiences, it is not formed in a vacuum. Beneath our beliefs, human beings have fundamental needs that arise from our inbuilt motivation to survive. Beliefs are constructed around the principle that these universal needs must be met. If you really want to understand human beings, you need to go one level deeper and get to grips with what lies at our core.

CHAPTER 7

Why Look at Core Needs, the *Why for All* Human Beings?

A cross nationalities, cultures, ages, religions – across people – there are certain fundamental issues that are important to us all, binding us together as human beings. Strangely, despite their significance, most of us struggle to articulate these core needs unless we make a determined effort to do so through deep reflection or therapeutic work. Yet, our deepest needs are so important, so fundamental to our existence, that they shape the people we become. That sounds dramatic, doesn't it? Well, it is. Understanding what drives us at such a basic level is part of developing our potential to become the richest human being we can be (and I don't mean that in a financial sense) because core needs provide the energy for change and urge us to accomplish our ambitions. As in the way of things, they can also be the greatest obstacle to achieving our life goals. Core needs are the fertile ground in which our belief system grows. They seep through our thoughts, values, style and behaviours. They are a part of us through and through and will not be left out. They are active in the thinking that runs under the radar of our awareness. They are our interpreters of the world, creating both the filters through which we see what is before us and the way in which we respond to it.

As a psychologist, I see my role as helping people work towards personal maturity, which is shorthand for learning to accept that we have the power to meet our core needs. We are not flotsam and jetsam, taken wherever the tide chooses; we have the ability to shape our own lives. This 'growing up', which may take us a lifetime to achieve, requires us first to understand what 'shape' we are trying to make, what needs we are striving to address.

What's this got to do with work?

Is getting deep into the realm of core needs out of your comfort zone? Am I asking too much of you as a manager to say that core needs should be on your agenda? Trust me. It's ok. Managers do need to consider core needs but not because they are meant to be therapists or counsellors or because they must understand the deeper machinations of everyone they meet. But consider this. If a manager is cognisant of the core needs of all people at a general level, he can ensure that his management style fosters an environment in which these needs have a greater chance of being met (or at least does not deliberately thwart them). As usual, this knowledge can also help us understand what we, you and I, need in order to be at our best.

What are the core needs?

The core needs can be labelled and sliced in different ways but I find a division into four most helpful.

- Human beings need to feel safe: *physically and emotionally*.

- Human beings need to feel that they matter: *that we have value*.

- Human beings need to feel that they belong: *that we are connected with others through shared identity*.

- Human beings need to feel change: *that in some way we move on and develop*.

You may feel that this is a straightforward list to get your management teeth around but these are only the headlines. What lies beneath is far more complex. Core needs are called 'core' because they are like the deep roots of a plant. They anchor the plant to its environment; they provide food and keep it alive. But the root is hidden. Its presence and its influence are forgotten because our attention is drawn to the great variety of foliage and blossom above ground. Nonetheless, the root and its side shoots (our beliefs and values), exert their influence 24/7.

Where does that leave us on core needs?

Most managers are accustomed to looking at, and evaluating, behavioural measures (the *what*) for managing performance. Similarly, many have experienced competency frameworks and psychometrics to consider underlying preferences and style (the *how*). Far fewer are familiar with values and beliefs (the *why*). Going even deeper into the inner workings of human beings is rarely on the manager's agenda. However, core needs are ubiquitous. They affect everything we do. In which case, isn't it worth giving them some thought?

What next?

If you want to be a true human being detective, you will need to stretch your thinking beyond the straightforward destinations of skills and knowledge into the pervasive world of core needs. If you're ready for the ride, the following chapters concern each of the deepest levels of 'why', starting with the need for safety.

CHAPTER 8
I Am Safe

Feeling safe is our bedrock. On it, we stand tall. In his well-known 'hierarchy of needs', Maslow[21] puts safety at the bottom of the stack, supporting all remaining needs. We are free to strive for our goals when we feel safe. Conversely, when we don't feel safe our attention is channelled into survival, whether physical or emotional. In extreme circumstances, lack of safety becomes a stop/go mechanism. If I fear for my life, it's unlikely that I will be able to work towards any goal other than my physical well-being. Where the threat to safety is less overpowering, it will split my attention as if one eye is kept on the threat while the other eye is focused on the rest of life's demands. We have binocular vision for a purpose – looking through two eyes provides depth and complexity. Looking through one eye gives us a limited view on life. Living without a sense of personal safety does that. It limits how we see and how we live life. But what does being safe mean?

Acceptable risk versus imposed threat

Few of us want to live as if encased in bubble-wrap because life without risk is dull. If we can stand on the edge of safety, we are safe enough. Seeing the risk, knowing it exists, provides an exhilaration that heightens our enjoyment but our threshold for safety, how close to that edge and how deep the drop we can tolerate, varies. You may be one of those people who can happily jump out of an aeroplane and freefall, juggle with knives and bet your last pair of trousers on a horse or, like me, you may prefer to take your risks in less extreme ways. The key to all these situations is that the degree of safety we choose is exactly that – a level that we choose. It's a totally different matter when the threat to our safety is imposed upon us and outside of our control. When the power to determine our destiny is held elsewhere, instead of exhilaration, we feel true fear.

The positive and negative value of fear

Clearly, there are times when a feeling of insecurity or overt fear is a valuable driver for self-preservation. It makes us escape from the situation (the best response to a threatening person holding a knife is to get out of his way fast) or avoid it in the first place (if a dark alley is dangerous, don't walk through it) or, if absolutely required, makes us act in defence whether physically, verbally or emotionally. Fear is an emotion with a rational purpose. It helps us recognise potential danger and act in the way best suited for survival.

Risk is part of work and, in many respects, that's a good thing. It can keep us focused, motivated, excited, willing to make an effort in order that we, and the enterprise we are part of, achieve our goals. The upside of risk is that the positive aspect of stress (known as eustress) can give a boost to our performance. It's the excitement that gets the adrenaline running before delivering a key presentation or the kick that gives us that extra something when our energy is flagging. The problem is that if the stress level rises beyond an individual's ability to cope with insecurity, stress turns into distress and the relationship with performance is reversed. Distress impacts negatively on our ability to deliver at our best.

Sources of threat

Our response to fear is rooted in the early stages of our evolution, when most threats were of a physical form and required a physical response. In a modern world, the category of 'threatening things' has become associated with a much broader range of far-reaching triggers including, but extending well beyond, the physical. Most of these triggers are not easily managed by our ancestral 'fight or flight' mechanisms, even though our bodies still respond physiologically in this way with significant implications for our health.

The visible and the invisible: Overt sources of threat can create a shared understanding of fear. Most people would feel afraid if faced with a hostile individual pointing a gun towards them – we would agree that the fear is well founded. Yet, many other triggers for insecurity are hidden from public view, leaving the individual struggling with their anxieties alone. Emotional abuse, bullying, mental health problems, financial worries, marital breakdown, conflict with colleagues or friends and job insecurity may be secret concerns but still have the power to gnaw away at our sense of safety with the potency of a threatening fist. Even when others are aware of the threat, they may be clueless about the degree of distress evoked by such actions.

Threats originating from outside the workplace: Most of us are skilled at putting on a mask for work, our 'work-face'. This is the self we choose to expose at the office and which keeps some aspects of our wider life private and in check. However, even if our work-face is well practised to the point of automatic, it does not stop the impact of our deeper-self interfering with how we behave with our colleagues and clients. Insecurity is difficult to hide and, whether we are aware of it or not, problems from our non-work life tend to sneak out from behind the mask and affect how we operate at work. As a manager, what might initially seem to be none of your business can still end up, albeit in a roundabout way, on your agenda.

Threats originating from within the workplace: Where shall I start? From the demands and complexity of individual tasks to difficulty in balancing competing priorities, keeping up to speed with technical developments and market changes, career dilemmas, the boss-subordinate relationship, competition with peers, issues with a team, conflict with other departments, stressful clients, the fit/non-fit with the prevailing culture, organisational change, home/work life tensions, the pressure from competition... phew! The list is long. There are sufficient sources of risk and insecurity at work to make an employee turn around at the front door and head straight home. Going to work can be extremely rewarding, stimulating and even fun but it's rarely a simple ride. When the positive stress it creates tips the balance to become painful anxiety, fear lurks closely in the shadows.

Specific threats versus pervasive insecurity: Insecurity may be specific to one situation (when I've just walked on stage with five hundred bored-looking people staring at me), just around the corner (the bully I work with is back from holiday tomorrow) or a more pervasive, generalised fear that is carried all the time (if I ever step out of line, I will get fired). All three can have a crippling effect on performance but the pervasive fear is usually the most damaging.

Vicarious threat: Such is our sensitivity to threat that our sense of personal safety can be affected by simply witnessing what happens to other people. Observing traumatic situations, even though there is no risk to our own safety, can leave a profound legacy in the form of long-term anxiety and fear. Unsurprisingly, post-traumatic stress is a common result for those who have been in extreme situations such as soldiers returning from war who have seen their comrades killed or injured. Events that are closer to home can have a similar impact. Those who have escaped a car crash unscathed while others were seriously hurt or who have witnessed a violent drunken brawl but were powerless to stop it can find disabling anxiety and fear follow. At work, too, though less dramatic perhaps, staff can be seriously distressed by witnessing the poor treatment of their colleagues. Following a round of redundancies, a section of the remaining employees may feel the unpleasant implications of 'survivor syndrome', fearful that they are next in line (If they can get the chop, why not me?).[22] It is a mistake to assume that those who are not directly affected by an action are not bruised by its wake.

What's this got to do with work?

Unfortunately, fear does more than raise our blood pressure. It restricts our choices. It's a highly potent emotion, hijacking our thinking. It bounces about at the forefront of our mind and spoils the view to other, more creative options. From the organisation's perspective, it deflects attention away from key goals. It impacts on performance and costs money or even lives, depending on the nature of the organisation. Recent scandals in the NHS, as documented in the report of the Francis Review,[23] have shown how a culture of fear in some hospitals prevented whistle-blowers being heard and serious performance issues being addressed. As a consequence, the patients at the end of this chain of fear were denied the care they deserved. Fear prevented people from speaking about the crimes of Jimmy Savile and his like. It kept actors quiet over the appalling behaviour of Harvey Weinstein. At the 2017 trial of three senior Tesco executives for fraud by abuse of power and false accounting, evidence was presented indicating that staff were bullied to 'cook the books', which, when it came to light, wiped £2 billion from the supermarket's value.[24]

On a smaller scale, consider these two examples. A talented senior executive with a fear of flying could cope with short flights but, when promoted to a global position requiring frequent long-haul trips, he feigned a heart problem to escape his role. He was prepared to lie about a serious health issue in preference to disclosing his fear. A young man with a fear of exams managed to pass through school and university successfully with the help of a support network made up of family and friends. When he took a secondment to a foreign country, he lost this support structure. Without it, the thought of his impending accountancy exams led to an upsurge in anxiety and frequent sick leave, which he attributed to a variety of fictional causes. It was some months before the real issue emerged. Both individuals managed to disguise their fears until their ability to cope broke down. With the correct support, they could have been helped to overcome their fears much sooner if they had felt it was safe to acknowledge them at work.

The personal and economic consequence of distress in the workplace is shown directly in the regular UK Government Health and Safety Executive (HSE) Labour Force Survey data (a household survey consisting of around 38,000 households across Great Britain). The 2015–16 survey[25] reported:

- In this period, stress accounted for 37% of all work-related ill health cases and 45% of all working days lost due to ill health.

- The total number of working days lost due to stress, depression and anxiety in 2015/16 was 11.7 million days. This equates to an average of 23.9 days lost per case.

- The main work factors cited by respondents as causing work-related stress, depression or anxiety were workload pressures, including tight deadlines, too much responsibility and lack of managerial support.

In addition to the Labour Force Survey, the HSE also collects data on work-related stress from general practitioners. The GP data is consistent with the Labour Force Survey data with regard to the causes of stress. Workload, lack of managerial support and organisational change were found to be the primary causative factors. None of this should be surprising. Feeling stressed and unsafe creates a damaging cocktail. It takes its toll on our emotions, our performance and our health. A sense of not being in control has long been shown to relate directly to the physiological correlates of stress (the physical fight or flight reaction), particularly the level of cortisol in the blood stream.[26] When too high, cortisol does damage in several insidious ways, meaning that if we feel unsafe our bodies suffer, we get sick and take valuable time away from our jobs.

The organisation as the cause of fear

Bullying and harassment at work are not rare occurrences. If you think the word 'bully' is too strong, try domineer, pressurise, browbeat, coerce, strong-arm, publicly criticise, exclude, isolate, insult, ridicule and so on. Whichever term you choose, the implication is one of intimidation through position or personal manner. Bad behaviour of this kind is not restricted to certain grades or roles. It can go from the bottom to the top. Certainly, I have seen some spectacularly bad behaviour from chief executives. It can be restricted to one or to a few people or be endemic in a culture. It crosses counties and continents. If you don't believe me, carry out an internet search on 'workplace bullying'. You won't be short of material to read.

There should be no place for an organisation that puts profit or achieving targets above treating human beings with respect, providing safe working conditions, using sound management practices, ethical employment arrangements and honest dealings with clients. Unfortunately, many organisations seem to slip through this net of respectability, as newspapers regularly report. While this slippery nature creates a temporary reprieve (and it may be lengthy one), an organisation that only succeeds through fear is, ultimately, a failing organisation. While the experience of bullying is a personal tragedy for the person on the receiving end, it can also be directly damaging to the organisation's productivity. Among other things, people who feel afraid tend to hunker down, hide behind the barricades, focus on themselves rather than their job, get sick and take time off or pack their briefcases and leave, taking their skills with them. This is costly. Employees are paid to do a job. If they are fearful, they are unlikely to be delivering the goods. There is an alternative, of course – an individual can always join the bullies if that's what it takes to get on. And that's just how toxic cultures develop. A toxic culture is more than costly. It can be dangerous, potentially threatening the organisation's viability. A study by Leicester University[27] following the Royal Bank of Scotland's collapse described a culture of 'economic violence' where leaders operated through the threat of destroying people's economic power by laying them off or forcing them to meet aggressive sales targets. The outcome for the bank, its employees and the British economy was not good. So, if the moral argument about bullying doesn't convince you that fear is a bad thing for the workplace, perhaps the economic one might.

External sources of insecurity

Just being alive opens the doors to worry, whether our concerns relate to major problems like health issues, marital breakdown, no money to pay the mortgage or chronic loneliness or to smaller problems like a neighbour who plays loud music late at night, making it impossible to sleep. If our coping resources are in credit, we may be able to brush such problems aside and their impact on us will be minimal. If our coping reserves are close to bankrupt, the smallest challenge can be a challenge too far. As noted earlier, willingly or unwillingly, people have always brought their home life worries with them to work even if they do not mention them openly. Imagine the diverse life circumstances of all the members of your organisation. Each day, some of those unique employees will be struggling to cope with something. If they begin to lose that struggle, it will eventually affect their work. Fortunately, many organisations now recognise the benefits of taking a more proactive role in offering support for specific problems, most notably around general health. In other areas, mental health in particular, there is still much to be done.

General ill health: Barring a terrorist campaign, a military invasion or a major food crisis, the most life-threatening event I am likely to encounter is ill health, physical or emotional. Human beings get sick and, despite dramatic improvements in health care and increased longevity, we still get sick. And sickness is expensive. A CBI survey in 2012 found that 'non-work-related illness and injury is by far the most widespread driver of employee absence, followed by post-operative recovery time' and 'the direct costs of absence alone amounted to over £14bn across the (*British*) economy in 2012'.[28]

To reduce this bill, organisations can do their bit by promoting healthier lifestyles. We know that a considerable degree of illness can be prevented or improved by adjusting our way of life, with weight loss, reducing alcohol intake, increasing exercise and stopping smoking at the top of the better-health list. The popularity of employee well-being programmes, employee assistance programmes, discounted gym membership and so on suggests that many employers do now recognise their part in this drive for health.

The 2014 Willis Eighth Annual Health and Productivity Survey Report, which gathered data from over 900 US companies,[29] found that while most (93%) considered healthier employees to be more productive, and 68% had some kind of programme to promote well-being, very few were actively measuring the impact of these initiatives on productivity. That organisations are not assessing the true value of such programmes is surely a missed opportunity. The indications are that, should they do so, they would be pleasantly surprised by the results. A review of available literature on workplace health promotion by the European Agency for Safety and Health at Work[30] concludes that the benefits from this kind of investment are significant in terms of increased production and productivity, job satisfaction and staff morale, with knock-on effects for improved customer service. It is also linked to a reduction in staff turnover and industrial accidents. Overall, programmes of this nature produce a safer and more profitable organisation to the benefit of individual employees and the enterprise overall. Despite this growing evidence, there seems to be some difficulty in getting people to believe it. The report finds one of the key barriers to implementing health promotion initiatives to be 'the misperception by employers and organisations that WHP (work health promotion) has limited or no benefits for the company, is too time-consuming, and is not their responsibility' (p5). It appears there is still some way to go to convince all CEOs that this broader definition of well-being and safety impacts on the bottom line.

Chronic conditions: You might be forgiven for thinking that scientific advances will cut the economic cost of ill health. Alas, this doesn't seem to be the case because with every 'swing' of improvement in health there is another 'roundabout' to deal with, particularly the rise in the number of people living with chronic conditions. In other words, the fact that we have, but don't die of, ill health is costly. There are now over two and a half million people living with, and beyond, cancer in the UK and this figure is set to rise to an estimated four million by 2030.[31] As the Macmillan Cancer Support report 'Cured - But at What Cost' (2013) states, being cured is often far from being well. Cancer can leave significant physical and mental conditions as a life-long residue. Their 2012 survey found:

> *The physical and emotional effects of cancer and its treatment are the two most common reasons why employees diagnosed with cancer give up work or change jobs. Almost half (48%) of those who do so say it's because they were not physically able to return to the same role, while one in three (33%) say they did not feel emotionally strong enough.*
>
> Macmillan Cancer Support, Cured –
> But at What Cost? *(2013)[32]*

The situation is similar for another major cause of ill health, heart disease.

> *The burden of coronary heart disease has subtly shifted over the last fifty years. Death rates for all age groups have consistently fallen since 1961, so that the risk of death from coronary heart disease for an adult in 2011 is equivalent to the risk of someone roughly fifteen years younger in 1961. But increases in life expectancy, combined with successful improvements in survival rates, have led to a large increase in the number of people in the UK who are suffering from coronary heart disease and its consequences. Over one and a half million people currently living in the UK have had a heart attack, and over two million people have angina and/or heart failure.*
>
> British Heart Foundation, Trends in Coronary Heart Disease, 1961–2011 *(2011)*[33]

We can expect that a significant proportion of any workforce will face serious health issues during their working lives and it is likely that staff with such health problems will need more than sick pay and time off. They will need support. Considerable energy and focus is needed to manage both the demands of work and the psychological drain of being unwell. Illness makes us vulnerable, anxious and maybe afraid. It changes our view of self and can do all kinds of things to our world view, to our sense of what matters to us most. At this testing time, what a human being needs is both another human being and a manager – the human being to provide empathy and support and the manager to deal with any practical adjustments needed in the role. Handing over the empathy bit to HR won't wash because human beings in difficulty need managers to bring humanity to their role as a constant; a manager who shows little genuine concern becomes a further source of worry and insecurity. If, as the statistics suggest, further advances in medical intervention result in more people living and working with serious conditions as a long-term way of life, organisations, leaders and managers will have to be more adept in accommodating their needs, beyond adjustments to working hours and leave. They will have to be better equipped to deal with emotion.

Mental health: A 2016 survey carried out for the CIPD[34] found that, of over 2,000 employees from across a range of organisations in the UK, three respondents in ten (31%) reported that they had experienced mental health problems while in employment. At the time of responding, 5% of those surveyed said their mental health was poor or very poor. Of this group, over half (54%) attributed their poor mental health to a combination of problems at work and outside work. Unsurprisingly, work can trigger mental health problems or make the impact of non-work issues worse. Less than half (46%) of the respondents reported that their organisation supported people who experience mental health problems very well or fairly well, while 20% reported that employees were not supported well or at all. The survey also showed that only 44% of employees would feel confident disclosing unmanageable stress or mental health problems to their current employer or manager.

It's the line manager who has the day-to-day responsibility for supporting an employee with a mental health problem, yet the survey found that just 10% of organisations provided training for managers to help them in this task. A manager who can spot the early signs, who can encourage the confidence needed for an individual to disclose their problem, who works with the individual to create a support plan and who follows this through with sensitive and caring interest, can make a considerable difference to the outcome for the individual and for his team. Sadly, as this survey indicates, all too often the organisational culture discourages people from asking for help and sometimes, even when they do, there isn't much on offer.

This is a sorry situation for the modern workplace as the impact of mental health issues on the individual, the organisation and the economy is substantial. In 2007, the Sainsbury Centre for Mental Health estimated the total cost to employers at nearly £26 billion each year.[35] That's equivalent to £1,035 for every employee in the UK workforce.

Caring for others: Concern for safety is not just about me. What's going on with my family and my friends affects me too. To feel comfortable enough to focus on my work priorities, I need to feel that the people and things that I hold dear are secure. We are familiar with the notion that working parents have to juggle their childcare and work demands. The use of the word 'juggle' is not used by accident with its implicit suggestion that, at any one time, something important that is not within our grasp is spinning. Today, increasing numbers of the workforce live two lives, as an employee and as a carer, with the so-called 'sandwich generation' looking after both children and elderly parents. And caring is a job in itself. Disabled children, older relatives and family members with mental health issues or a physical illness exist in a wide range of families, irrespective of social and economic background. General parenting aside, the 2011 census reported that approximately 5.8 million people provide unpaid care in England and Wales, representing just over one tenth of the population and indicating a 10% increase on the previous census, in 2001. Although many carers are talented at compartmentalising the psychological load of their different roles, it's difficult to feel safe and in control when the well-being of loved-ones is at stake. As the external support available to help with caring is limited, carers can quite easily be left teetering on the precipice of not coping. It's only to be expected that this dual role will take its toll somewhere and that somewhere may well be at work. After all, we are only human beings not superhuman beings.

How to damage 'I am safe'

Sometimes, it's easier to spot when things are going wrong than when they're on the right track. Hence, before looking at the important 'to-dos' needed to increase a sense of safety, here are a few 'don'ts'. I'm sure you wouldn't dream of doing any of the following but I'm also sure you will have seen some of these behaviours or, alas, been on the receiving end of them.

Don't care: Showing indifference to an individual's stress, health problems or other worries reinforces the view that you have no interest in them as a human being. If I feel I am valueless to you, then I will worry that you might discard me without a thought.

Make assumptions about how people feel or think: On a par with showing no interest is assuming that you know exactly what's going on in another person's head and heart. You may share similar experiences with others, you might even share some similar feelings, but you can't truly understand another's perspective until you listen to it. If you make assumptions and get it wrong, you risk coming across as patronising, arrogant or downright insulting.

Be a bully: Use your position, your authority, your height, your loud shouty voice or your choice vocabulary to intimidate people. Surveys that seek to find out the extent of bullying in the workplace tend to count the number of victims not the number of bullies but there can't be one without the other. Someone is doing the bullying. Is it you? I mean that seriously. Is it you? Think about this carefully. We are not always fully aware of the consequences of our words and actions.

Don't tell people what's going on: Keeping people in the dark is a great way of making them feel uncomfortable. A conversation between senior people held behind closed doors sets the rumour mill turning and, for some reason, rumours tend to err on the negative rather than the positive side. If you leave a communication void, expect it to get filled up – with worries.

Make decisions without explaining how you arrived at them: If I have no rational explanation for what you've done, I can't feel safe about what might happen next.

Try to hide the truth: Covering up a situation rarely works. Part of the story leaks out and the twist it acquires is often of the worst-case variety than a more balanced, truthful reality.

Breach trust: Say one thing and do another. Break a confidence. Talk about someone behind their back. Oh, it's so easy to do and so difficult to put right after the event.

Tell people where they're going wrong without telling them what they do right: Emphasising problems without recognising strengths is a sure way to make people feel unsafe. Similarly, giving no guidance on how to improve a problem leaves human beings feeling confused and stranded.

Create employment contracts that give no financial security: If you treat me as dispensable and I have no other job available, I will live with constant insecurity.

Collude with, or promote, unhealthy lifestyles: Sure, it's ok to drink and eat to excess when on company business, to work long, long hours, not to take a holiday, to get stressed out. Provided you're doing your job, it's none of my business. Or is it?

Be a fear carrier: One way to stoke up insecurity is to let your own fears permeate through your words and actions. You may think that you hide your worries well but most people wear transparent clothes when it comes to anxiety. Even if you don't speak about your concerns, your body language will give you away. And fear begets fear.

How to strengthen 'I am safe'

If those are the 'no-no's, here are the 'musts' to boost your team members' feeling of safety. Your aim should not be to produce a comfort blanket that reduces any sense of risk or edge to work but rather to instil confidence in your team that they have the personal resources needed to cope with the challenges they face. Your support to help them in this endeavour should be crystal clear.

Know your own safety needs: Think about what makes you feel secure or insecure. When you feel under threat, how do you react? How does this reaction then impinge on your staff (because it will)? Do you create motivating stress or unhealthy distress? Can you address your safety needs in a different way? What demands do you face in and out of work that involve risk or threat? Who gives you support when you need it? Understanding your own need for safety may be the most important action you take to increase the sense of 'I am safe' in your team.

Make space and time for people to tell you their concerns: Spend time with your people and get to know them as human beings, not just as people who perform tasks. You don't have to be best friends. You don't need to know their mother's maiden name or what they ate for breakfast but you should know what motivates them at work, what switches them on and what switches them off. You should aim to develop a relationship in which there is sufficient trust and respect that individuals will feel comfortable telling you when something is awry or, when they are not explicit in this, your management antenna can detect it. Then, your human being self should offer a genuine opportunity to talk, not a few rushed minutes at the coffee machine. The individual may decline your invitation – that's their choice – but you can leave the door ajar if they change their mind. To be open to this kind of conversation, you may first need to improve your own level of comfort dealing with emotion, to get past any sense of embarrassment. You will need to have the patience to hear out concerns and recognise that one conversation is unlikely to fix a long-term problem. You will have to suspend judgement. In short, you will need to be both manager and human being.

Keep reinforcing value to those who need it: The better you know your people, the easier it will be for you to identify those who need a high level of reassurance and those who don't. You may be tempted to say that feeling insecure 'is their problem not mine' but if insecure people are left in the grip of their anxieties they can create problems that, at a later date, take considerably more of your time to manage than small amounts of planned input upfront. Find out what information individuals need to feel they are delivering a good job then be as clear as you can in stating your expectations. In other words, tell them what they need to know in order to feel comfortable. Remember that, if you are someone who dislikes being micromanaged, you probably manage others with a light touch too but be aware that there are those who absolutely need the more involved style of management that you find stultifying. Alternatively, if you are a manager with a strong need for security, consider that you may be stifling some of your team members with too much supervision when they need more autonomy to feel trusted and safe. The solution to getting this right is to make sure you get to know your people as individual human beings.

Make your team a harassment free zone: Make your expectations about respectful behaviour explicit and ask your team to commit to them formally. Create a confidential process through which people can report if they are being intimidated in any way. Pick up on unacceptable behaviour and let your team see that you mean business about this. A word of warning. If you see bad behaviour, be careful how you treat the perpetrator. Blast the behaviour but don't demonise the individual. This won't help them change. Coach them to understand their behaviour or call on specialised help if the problem is severe.

Communicate: Keep communication channels open and talk to your people even when there's no news to tell. If you communicate through a cascade arrangement, don't assume that messages get through. I'm sure you know the game of Chinese whispers, where a message changes form each time it's passed on. Check out that your communication isn't suffering a similar fate.

Be straight with people: If there is bad news, be honest and give information early on. People are more likely to trust you if they feel included and taken into your confidence. If you decide to hold information back, double-check why you're doing so. What's the risk of being more open? Weigh this against the risk of holding back. We are often more cautious than needed.

Respect confidentiality: If you think you are about to be told something that you know you can't keep to yourself, stop the conversation. Give the individual the choice of whether to continue or not before it's too late. If you break someone's trust by disclosing a confidence, accidentally or otherwise, you will have a long, uphill climb to regain trust and, while you're climbing, insecurity will be doing its worst with their performance. This confidentiality clause covers what you say in the restaurant, on the train or at home as well as what is said in the office. Many of us are not discreet. We intend to be but somehow those confidences just slip out – think mobile phones and train carriages: need I say more?

Acknowledge stress that originates outside the workplace: If you know your people well, you will recognise when an individual is overdrawn on their capacity to cope, when manageable stress has changed to distress. When you spot this happening, get extra advice and help so that you can give support sooner rather than later. Flexibility in work arrangements and timely support can often prevent a problem developing into a crisis and allow a valued employee to continue delivering their role.

Understand your organisation's policies for supporting people in ill health and promoting well-being: If, in your opinion, these policies are not good enough or are not lived out in practice, campaign for something better. Review the expectations you give to your team about working long hours or at weekends, answering emails in non-work time and taking holidays.

Encourage healthy lifestyles: You may feel that employee well-being initiatives require strategic change beyond your level of influence but don't settle for that. You can create a healthy team just by encouraging your colleagues to use the stairs rather than the lift or to take a regular walk from the office and see the sun when it's out. So, put on your training shoes and head outside to soak up some vitamin D. It's a great team-building opportunity. You can encourage people to take a lunch break rather holding a sandwich in one hand and tapping a keyboard with the other. Invite speakers to discuss health matters with your staff. Challenge a culture of long hours and presenteeism for its own sake. Role model living your life as a human being as well as an employee.

What next?

Feeling safe gives us the freedom, confidence and space to focus our attention on satisfying our other core needs, a sense of *I matter*, *I belong* and *I change*. If you're feeling comfortable, it's time for a whistle-stop tour of each one.

CHAPTER 9

I Matter

A s we arrive, gasping for our first lungful of air, the communities we join can be poles apart geographically, socially, physically, genetically and economically but, however great these differences, we share one common value. We are all equal human beings. No one is born of more value than another. With time, our run of life may send us on different paths but whatever befalls us our common value remains, whether prince or bag-lady, rock star or politician, homemaker or astronaut. We all matter. This doesn't mean our behaviour is of equal value in terms of its contribution. There is certainly good and bad in behaviour but differences in wealth, position, lineage, IQ, appearance, ability and career, by themselves, do not alter the fundamental equality of human beings.

The principle of equal value is not science. The United Nations Universal Declaration of Human Rights may start with the words 'All human beings are born free and equal in dignity and rights' but there is no list of facts to prove it. It's something you simply accept or don't. If you're in the latter camp, you may as well park this book and use your time doing whatever it is you do because it'll only annoy you. If, though, you accept this premise readily, then I have two questions for you.

1. How easy is it to believe that you matter? Yes, *you*.

2. How easy is it to believe that others matter as much as you?

Got the answers? Think about them as you read this chapter. They may not be as straightforward as they first appear.

Where does a sense of self-worth come from?

Our early years are critical in helping us develop a sense that we matter. To survive as a helpless baby, it is essential that we are protected. Parents put considerable time and resources into this protection. Why do they do this? Because they value their child. The natural attachment that occurs between parents and their children helps to seal this sense of value. The young child is aware that he is the centre of his parents' universe and feels secure as a result. As the child grows up, he begins to challenge the ties that have held him safe and to make his own way, fuelled by the confidence that he has worth.

As anyone with children will know, helping offspring create this inner self-belief is not an easy task. Children are extraordinarily sensitive to events that have the potential to question their value. What's more, their level of sensitivity is not constant – a trivial matter can make a major impact and be remembered for years afterwards, while a major issue may go no further than skin deep. Parenting is difficult because an adult's perspective is unlikely to be the same as their child's; what makes a splash with us may not raise a ripple with them, and vice versa. Children create a personalised and individual understanding of their world.

Every childhood leaves its mark in the form of a set of beliefs on which our inner self-image is built, beliefs that validate our sense of worth and beliefs that question it. As noted previously, because these beliefs are laid down early on, as we age it is easy to lose track of the evidence on which they were constructed. After a while, they just are. Then, as we grow, life adds to these beliefs, confirming or challenging them with its combination of rosettes, 'wet fish in the face' moments and everything in-between.

The answer to *how easy is it to believe that you matter?* is – sometimes it's easy and sometimes it's not. We all have a sense of our own value and we all have doubts about it. I would be surprised if you didn't have times when you questioned your own worth because, in my many years as a psychologist, I have met few people who truly accept their own value, and those who do have worked hard to achieve this. It takes a long time to be fully at ease with oneself, more time than some individuals ever have. Fortunately, total acceptance isn't required to lead a happy and fulfilling life. A reasonable degree of acceptance is good enough. What's more, those self-doubts can be very useful.

What's this got to do with work?

As believing that we matter is a core need, one of the motivational forces of our being, it has considerable influence over our behaviour, for good and for not so good, even though we are often unaware of its hold over us. Therefore, as a manager, if you do things that impact negatively on this core need, you do more than sap the person's energy and commitment for the job. You risk letting loose a panoply of behaviours that are disruptive or damaging. Appreciating the importance of helping people feel valued is an important aspect of a manager's role.

Uncertainty about our value, that we matter, is particularly potent in shaping our behaviour. It can feel like having an empty space, or hole, at our centre. The greater the uncertainty, the greater the hole that needs to be filled and the stronger the urgency to find the often indefinable piece that is missing. To ease this unpleasant state, we look for something to fill the empty space. And what do we fill it with? A form of proof.

Whether we realise it or not, we are all on the hunt for proof that we are as good as the next man or woman. Even a tiny baby looks for signals that it's loved. As adults, we prefer not to be that gushy about it and talk not about love but more about the search for respect or recognition. Whatever we call it, we're still after the proof that we matter. Once found, we use this evidence to convince ourselves and others of our value. When the need is particularly strong, the hunt for proof can infiltrate all aspects of life – work, sport, voluntary activities, hobbies, our love life, our friendships and even our parenting.

The effects of this search can be bad or good depending on the circumstances. It can, for instance, be a major driver in our work life, keeping us on our toes, motivating us to try harder and giving us the energy to keep going when times are tough. Management books frequently talk about the drive for achievement. Recruiters look for it. Bosses reward it. Promotions are decided on it. The world of work likes people who are hungry for challenge, hungry for proof. In many ways, the energy that comes from the need to prove our own value creates the impetus for a thriving career and a significant contribution in the workplace.

On a personal level, however, the benefits may be less clear cut. The drive for proof can be costly because collecting proof requires effort. What's more, proof, even vast quantities of it, rarely satisfies the desire for recognition. Somehow, it doesn't have the right something that's required to fill that empty space. Indeed, depending on our stage of life, it can even make the space grow wider and deeper. Proof also has a strange trick of changing form. What seems to be rock-solid evidence becomes more questionable when it's in the palm of our hand. The positive feeling derived from achieving a desired promotion, new job or pay rise can lose its impact quickly, leaving those with a need for proof back on the hunt for the next promotion, job and so on. Alternatively, proof may be reclassified as not really proof at all along the lines of 'Yes, it's good that I achieved that but, now I come to think of it, it's not that special'. For some, this endless search can feel like running a race in which the finishing line keeps moving. Just when the winning tape is in sight, it disappears into the distance. Running an endless race is fine when you're fit and keen to run but after a while it gets tiring and painful. When we question whether we matter at our core, all the certificates, medals, promotions, commendations, sales wins and one-ups on our peers cannot answer the question 'do I matter?'.

While an inner uncertainty about worth leads to emotional discomfort for the individuals concerned, it can also create an uncomfortable life for those around them. Despite their achievements, people with a strong need for proof can make difficult colleagues, bosses and staff. Their behaviour can range from the mildly irritating to downright destructive and have significant consequences for the organisation. It can take the form of demands for attention and recognition, overly competitive behaviour or negativity when it seems the evidence of their value is missing (even if it isn't). It can be skewed towards showing that 'I am more valuable than you' or lead a stressed and critical boss to make unreasonable demands of his staff who then feel they can never satisfy his requirements. At the other extreme, it can also make a manager reluctant to take risks for fear that failure will further undermine his self-worth.

The proof conundrum

The reason the hunt for proof doesn't sate our hunger is that, at root, no amount of evidence can prove value. Throw everything into that bottomless pit and it will never fill up. Accepting that we matter is not about proof but a matter of acceptance because there is nothing to prove in the first place.

This chapter began with the obvious statement that all people are born equal and worthy of love. It follows then that every child deserves to be valued whether the people around do so or not. When we search for proof of our value, we are searching for something that relates to a time lost to our memories, when we needed to feel secure and loved by our parents. We needed to know that they cared about us no matter what. This is our evolutionary heritage, an inbuilt need to ensure our survival. Our search for proof relates right back to the child we once were, trying to work out how to behave to get the affection that signals we will be kept safe.

Herein rests the conundrum. Unless we grasp the initial truth that we deserved care and affection, without having to do or 'be' anything other than ourselves, then all the proof in the world is aimed at the wrong equation. It's trying to solve the wrong problem. We deserved to be accepted and loved just for being us. Without proof.

If that's difficult to accept for yourself, think of the people you love most in life, particularly your own children if you have them. I'm certain that you believe these special people deserve to be valued regardless of their achievements, i.e. regardless of proof. You love and value them without proof.

Coming to terms with this view of self-worth is immensely freeing. It allows us to choose what we do rather than be driven by hidden and erroneous beliefs about how we 'must' be (remember the tyranny of the musts?). Even if our early years were painful and we did not receive the care and value we deserved, leaving us questioning our value, they do not have to define us now.

Too much need for proof – achievement overdrive

Getting to the top of an organisation is tough. Overtaking others who are competing for a diminishing number of roles in the pyramid of hierarchy takes effort and determination, personal sacrifice (or that of your family) and compromise of other values. Only those with a powerful drive to achieve make it. Less-driven folk either choose to take a different path because the sacrifice isn't worth it or are they passed by, or even trodden on, by those with a higher level of determination. Of course, ability is important too but without the drive to succeed, it is unlikely to be enough. Consequently, the cumulative need for proof of 'I matter' increases the higher up an organisation we look. In the top few leadership levels, it's often so strong it can be overpowering, literally. The result is a layer of senior folk that is skewed in style: a highly driven and sometimes aggressive group of people with a predominance of competition over collaboration, political play rather than open communication, demand for external status as a means of recognition and, quite frequently, demonstrations of bad behaviour ranging from domineering to bullying. Of course, today's senior leaders are unlikely to recognise this picture. They will argue that their actions and decision-making are based purely on rational, analytical reasoning, firmly from the 'computer'. Few are likely to acknowledge that their 'hearts' are leading them just as strongly.

You may feel that I'm over-egging the pudding a little here. Not all senior teams are the same, that is true, but many are and it's a dangerous scenario. It can lead to serious errors of judgement. Most dangerous perhaps is when the need to prove equal worth is substituted with a blind belief in being of 'greater worth' (along the lines of 'to feel valuable, I have to believe I am better, more able, than others'). The actions leading to the financial crisis at the Bank of Scotland in 2008 provide an example of how a senior team, and a CEO in particular, can create a distorted bubble of self-belief through an erroneous sense of infallibility.

> *It is difficult, from the evidence now available, to*
> *be certain how aspects of RBS's management,*

governance and culture affected the quality of its decision-making, but the Review Team's analysis prompts the following questions, in addition to the conclusion about the ABN AMRO bid:

- *Whether the Board's mode of operation, including challenge to the executive, was as effective as its composition and formal processes would suggest.*

- *Whether the CEO's management style discouraged robust and effective challenge.*

- *Whether RBS was overly focused on revenue, profit and earnings per share rather than on capital, liquidity and asset quality, and whether the Board designed a CEO remuneration package which made it rational to focus on the former.*

- *Whether RBS's Board received adequate information to consider the risks associated with strategy proposals, and whether it was sufficiently disciplined in questioning and challenging what was presented to it.*

> *Financial Services Authority*, The Failure of the Royal Bank of Scotland *(2011)*[36]

What's to be done?

How about compulsive therapy for senior leaders? Well, there's a thought. Perhaps not, there isn't enough time. The answer is simpler than that. Greater awareness, more openness, identifying and acknowledging personal interest and identifying bad behaviour when it happens are all actions a board, trustees, colleagues, staff, shareholders and customers can employ to call senior executives to account. We need to get frank about what's going on around the senior management table and give others permission to say so without risk of sanction. Those in a position of scrutiny need a new checklist of areas to review when looking at senior level performance. More attention also needs to be given to how we select and promote people to senior roles. As noted previously, it's a common failing to recruit in our own likeness and even the most sophisticated selection processes can be twisted to make this happen. Selection is not science. Above all, there is an assumption that high achievement drive is a prerequisite for top jobs without questioning what this achievement is for – the individual's needs, those of the organisation or both?

What's this got to do with work?

As I have mentioned before, it's not a manager's responsibility to get an individual's (let alone the CEO's) core needs into shape. The core needs that we carry in adulthood are the result of a lifetime's experiences and you cannot, even if you want to, sort that lot out on your own and it's not your business to either. That's down to the individual.

Alas, this doesn't let you off the hook because, wherever your staff are on their personal scale of self-worth, you can make them feel *more* or *less* valuable from the moment they join your team. Unfortunately, it seems much easier to push people towards the *less* than the *more* end of this scale, particularly if we give little thought to the impact our actions make on human beings rather than on human resources. Many a manager has unintentionally made a significant dent in another's sense of value. But, if you are willing to give it some thought and time, it's quite straightforward to boost self-esteem and reap the rewards for so doing.

How to damage 'I matter'

The key requirement for 'I matter' is that word 'respect' again. The easiest way to diminish a person's sense of value is to deny them respect and, in the pressured environment of work where, as a manager, meeting my goals depends on my staff meeting theirs, that's extraordinarily easy to do. You don't have to be the boss from Hades to score highly on the diminishing front. Why? Because you too have doubts about your self-worth. And so do I and so does the man in the next office and the woman I sat opposite on the train this morning. Everyone has a degree of doubt about their value and, unless we are self-aware, we can allow our doubts to play out on others in a variety of unhelpful ways. When a manager's need to prove his self-worth is gripping him tightly, expect a behavioural repertoire where someone somewhere will feel the sharp edge of disrespect. So, watch out for the following 'no-nos' as they're easy to slip into and very damaging to a sense of 'I matter' for those on the receiving end.

Don't listen to people: Look vaguely in their direction while thinking of the next meeting or how you will impress your boss or where you're going for lunch. Pay lip service to their ideas. Show your indifference. Assume *we* know best and *our* way is the only way.

Don't use the skills and talents an individual possesses: Avoid giving people the opportunity for decision-making when they are capable of doing so. Keep them in roles below their ability and deny them development that would help them progress. Don't let them learn from you. Delegate the worst tasks only.

Deliberately treat others as if they are unequal: Discriminate on grounds of race, gender, sexuality, age, disability or religion. Use language that damns the person rather than challenges their behaviour.

Treat people as children: Avoid being frank and honest about an individual's position in the organisation; behave like a parent or schoolteacher rather than an equal adult.

Make a big 'to-do' about mistakes but ignore achievement: Create hell for those around you when deadlines are missed, when errors occur, when something doesn't go quite as planned but keep quiet during the rest of the time when everything runs smoothly.

Play the king: Behave as if you are more important because you have a grander job title, a bigger desk, a bigger salary or a bigger anything.

Take the credit for others' achievements: Put me-the-manager forward as the representative of the team even though others have done the work. Willingly take the glory for a team success.

Show obvious disrespect: Cancel meetings to see someone more important. Take phone calls rather than keep your attention on the person you are with (tell me, who doesn't do this these days?). Shout, swear, use demeaning language and generally behave like a prat.

How to strengthen 'I matter'

Start with yourself. To fully accept the worth of others and strengthen their sense of 'I matter', we have first to get our thinking straight that we matter too.

Value yourself: When we are on the hunt for proof that we matter, we are too busy with our own needs to focus on bolstering the needs of others. onsider whether you truly value yourself. This doesn't mean ignoring weak spots, exaggerating capabilities and generally walking with a swagger. Accepting our value is about acknowledging both our strengths and the not-so-flattering aspects of our make-up yet still recognising that, at a fundamental level, we matter just as much as the next John or Joan. If you have doubts, and I suspect you may, think about where they come from, the *why*, and challenge the old reasoning on which they are based. If those doubts are significant, you will probably need some help to do this. From experience, I know that much coaching work centres on helping managers and leaders get a clearer perspective on their worth.

By acknowledging our value as a given, we remove the self-imposed pressure of a never-ending search for proof. This frees our energy, our attention and our time and, as a more effective manager, it allows us to work for other ambitions. It allows us to recognise whether the behaviour aimed at proving our value really serves this purpose or, through its unwanted consequences, it does the opposite. Think of the manager who always has to be seen as knowing better than his staff. Unless he is truly brilliant, his team are likely to regard him as a fool. Letting go of the burden of proof allows us to have a broader and clearer perspective, that is, one no longer clouded by misinformation drawn from unhelpful beliefs about how we 'should be'. It allows us to build a stronger sense of 'I matter' in others because to do so no longer detracts from our own sense of worth. Value becomes about win–win not win–lose. Perversely, when we accept ourselves for who we are, our blemishes and our talents, we are often able to achieve more than when held in the grip of a need for proof.

Be generous: If you have confidence in your value, you will be able to share the limelight and be generous with your praise. Most achievements are created through the effort and skill of a range of people. Give recognition to all and let your team take the plaudits even if you must step back to do so. Praise the effort made towards an end goal even when things don't go to plan. Many factors outside of a team's control can make success difficult or even impossible to achieve so the 'trying' must be applauded even if the end result was not what was hoped for. When success seems to be elusive, remind your people of what they do well. We all benefit from reminders about our capability.

Relish diversity and uniqueness: Look for the specific talents of the individual members of your team. Value this diversity and use the range of skills and styles available to you to boost the creativity and adaptability of your area. Difference is good! Seek to understand people 'in the round'. Respect their interests, their life outside work, their beliefs and their personal goals. If you don't know the talents your staff possess outside their everyday work role, you don't know them well enough.

Seek to understand: When something goes wrong, it's tempting to blame people rather than situations. Most people set out to do a good job. When things go wrong, it's rarely their intention that this should happen. Be wary of your first reaction, particularly if it's anger – your computer won't be working well when you're in a rage. Allow your emotional response to subside then employ your critical thinking to understand the aspects of the heart and the computer that lie behind performance issues. When you investigate problems, let your people know that you want to understand the situation rather than judge the person. 'I didn't like what you did' is very different from 'I don't like you'. Above all, allow people to retain their self-respect in difficult moments. If an exam is failed, a sale is lost, profits are down, a presentation does not go as hoped, a client is unhappy or targets are not reached, nothing is gained by demeaning your team. Your people will feel bad enough about what has happened and their sense of 'I matter' will have taken a knock. The manager's role is to build this back up so that they have the confidence and energy to improve.

Encourage collaboration: Set tasks that deliberately draw on collaboration rather than competition within a team. Show team members that they need each other if they, and the organisation, are to achieve.

Celebrate success: Tell your people that their contribution matters, that *they* matter. We do too little of this. Celebration doesn't have to be a party and doesn't need to be expensive. It can be as simple as a bag of doughnuts or a word of congratulations in a meeting. Much of work is serious but that doesn't mean we have to be miserable about it. Fun is not a rude word.

What next?

You're ready for the day. You woke up feeling confident about yourself; you know you've got just what the world needs to make a difference. You've checked out the neighbourhood and it looks like a safe place to strut your stuff. So, you step out. *Look out, world, I'm coming!*

Oh. There's no one there.

Let's talk about the need to belong.

CHAPTER 10

I Belong

We all have moments when we crave to be left alone, when the demands of other people are too exhausting to manage, when another meeting, another visitor, another anything, is one 'another' too far. But imagine the opposite. Imagine being alone, when you are free to do as you wish but there is no one to share it with. No one to talk to, no one to argue with, no one to laugh with, no one to care about what happens to you. This is the stuff of which nightmares are made. This sense of being alone, dislocated from others or cast adrift from society is not rare. Families grow up and move on. Partners die. People retire. Active and busy lives can become quiet existences unless a concerted effort is made to create new, or strengthen old, networks.

Aloneness is not a natural state. We are social animals and we have a strong need to belong. In evolutionary terms, this makes sense. By staying connected with others, our chances of survival (and thereby safeguarding our genetic line) are increased. Hence, the need to be joined in some way to our fellow human beings is a fundamental human need that serves several purposes.

- Belonging[37] helps confirm our identity. By belonging, we accept common features or activities as part of 'us'.

- Belonging gives us security. It provides us with allies whom we hope will support us.

- Belonging gives us an anchor. Because we are anchored to one group, we have the confidence to explore beyond it. Like a piece of elastic, our 'belonging' can pull us back to safety.

- Belonging provides guidance and boundaries about how to behave; it provides a template to follow.

Over a lifetime, we belong to a range of different social groups. Some are local – our family, friends, school, neighbourhood, place of worship, work, sports teams and so on. Others are more distant – our religion, nationality, skin colour, sexuality, political party. The possibilities for the membership of groups and sub-groups (e.g. my best friends at school versus the rest) and groups that overlap (the people who support the political party I support and who live in my county) are endless. In addition, our membership isn't static and can change with time (e.g. when children grow up and leave school, our membership of the school parents' group is lessened or broken). Our satisfaction with belonging can also vary. We may grow to challenge the boundaries of a group, regarding them as restrictions rather than helpful guides. We may simply change our mind and prefer to belong to a different group or ideology. Many of us change our political affiliation over time. In extreme circumstances, when we feel we cannot leave a group, our belonging can become a burden.

We can only belong to one group by not belonging to another

Do you remember learning 'set theory' in maths? It mostly involves drawing and colouring intersecting circles, a light relief from complex algebra. It goes something like this.

What's in circle A belongs to set A. What's in circle B belongs to set B. What's in circle C belongs to set C, and so on. Where the circles overlap, well, heck, it's obvious: they belong to both or all sets. Let circle A be my family. Let circle B be my workplace, and let circle C be the fans of my favourite sports team.

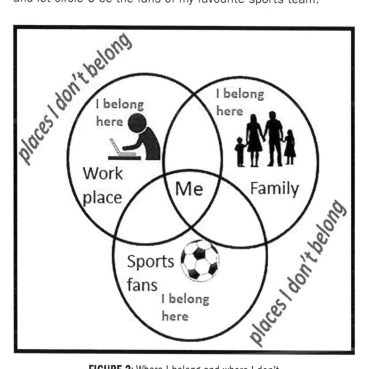

FIGURE 2: Where I belong and where I don't

I will lie where all three circles intersect. If my sister works with me and supports my sports team too, she'll be keeping me company.

The interesting and often neglected feature here is what lies outside the circles – that is, everybody else. Those who do not belong to my sets. In this example, they are people who don't work with me, are not my family, and who don't support my team. They occupy the space in the rest of the rectangle that is not part of A or B or C. This space exists, so it's part of something, but it's not the part to which I belong.

Does that matter? Well it might

Perhaps we don't care about our 'not belonging' (the groups we are not a part of). For instance, the fact that others support a different sports team may be completely unimportant to me. Let them do their own thing provided they leave me alone. Then again, in some instances, perhaps we do care. The fact that those fans are chanting and waving their scarves because their team beat mine may be irritating or cause resentment or downright anger. Or it may make me feel superior – however good their chants, mine are better. Or it may make me feel inferior – they're lucky, their team always wins. Alternatively, I might be fed up with my team and decide it's time to switch sides but worry about how many friends I will lose in the process.

Not belonging is the consequence of belonging to something else. There is no escape from this. The boundaries we create to keep the 'not belonging' out can be great indeed and often pass through generations of people, continents of space and centuries of time. It's this 'not belonging' that is the root of discord, disagreement, prejudice, hatred and ultimately war in a world where those who are not like us can easily become the enemy. The stronger the boundary, the deeper the identity within a group and the greater the barrier to those outside it.

Differences in skin colour, race, religion, age, education, gender, sexuality, disability, economic status and pretty much any aspect of human variety can become the basis for a boundary to keep people in or out of belonging. Recent world events have shown how a sense of being emotionally within or outside a group can influence the political agenda in a major way. This is particularly so in countries where social change in the form of migration has occurred faster than many of the existing group members can assimilate. US President Donald Trump's promise to build a wall to keep non-Americans out and Britain's vote for Brexit both involve a retrenching of the boundaries on belonging. The circles in the set theory diagram of the USA and Britain have got smaller. Those who voted for this change feel a strengthened sense of being American or British. Those who voted against it feel a loss of being part of a wider community in which they had felt at home, for one man's belonging is another man's not belonging.

A fascinating aspect of this kind of extreme change is the emotional underpinning of the decision-making process involved. The campaigns for both major events pulled at the heartstrings of voters as much as, if not more, than they fed rational data to their computers. Warning lights should flash at this point. History has shown that those who aim to manipulate human beings through their need to belong play a dangerous game indeed.

What's this got to do with work?

Despite the major events happening on the world stage, our most important place for belonging relates to our family. Coming in a close second, however, is the workplace because we spend much of our valuable time there. As a manager, you have to face facts. Your actions can either help meet this need or thwart it. If you leave the development of a sense of belonging to your team to chance, you risk seeing your staff choosing to put their emotional feet in another circle, to belong to something else that takes their fancy. Their bottom may be sitting on a chair in your office but their heart and mind may be elsewhere.

It was not unusual for those of my parents' generation to work for the same organisation for their entire career. My father was employed by the BBC for over forty years. At the time he joined, the deal the organisation made with its staff was the offer of security of employment in return for performance and loyalty. For my father, this loyalty has continued even though the BBC has changed beyond recognition. His strong sense of belonging, demonstrated through lasting friendships and active involvement in formal networks, has continued for some thirty years past the day of his last pay cheque. He is still a BBC man.

Loyalty is perhaps easiest to understand as a willingness to put the organisation's needs as equal to, if not ahead, of one's own. In a military setting, this can mean putting your life at risk for others. Fortunately, for most of us, loyalty is less dramatic but it still requires thinking, feeling and behaving in a way that supports the common interests of the team and organisation. Unfortunately for today's managers, creating the sense of belonging that fosters loyalty isn't easy in our new world of work. My father's career path is now almost unheard of. Membership of teams, departments and whole organisations is transient. What we belong to shifts and, sometimes, shifts at speed. This movement and uncertainty makes the emphasis on belonging particularly important for a manager even if it's a tough job to achieve. Belonging provides the handrail for staff to hold on to when the movement gets too unsettling. If there's no handrail, when the going gets rough someone, a few or everyone will fall.

Is loyalty a good thing? Belonging to an organisation's culture

Culture can be contagious. New into an organisation, looking at the behaviour of some employees, you may have said, 'I will never act like that' but after a while you may have found yourself doing just the thing you disliked. At that point, you have moved from being an onlooker of 'them' to becoming 'one of us'. When leaders talk about inculcating a specific type of culture, what they really mean is generating a sense of belonging where members share similar values, approaches to work and commitment that, in combination, will make employees more productive. This high degree of loyal belonging, where we are all 'one of us', is generally regarded as a good thing as it indicates:

- a willingness to focus effort in a given direction even if team members have not had a say in choosing this path;

- sufficient trust in leaders that, should a change in direction be needed, employees will go with it;

- retention of key employees because to leave an organisation to which an individual feels loyal, particularly to join a competitor, is not undertaken lightly. It involves more than a change of office; it requires is a change of heart.

But how high is high? Total loyalty is unhealthy for both the individual and the organisation. At an individual level, submission to an organisation's belief system can mean a considerable compromise of one's own values and beliefs. That submission comes at a cost with independence of thought and even moral perspective overridden. That may not matter if the organisation's culture has a noble nature that supports the well-being of all its stakeholders and fosters sustainability but if it leads all the company lemmings to fall off a cliff together, it would be handy if one or two were willing to shout 'stop'. Perhaps recent disasters in the banking sector could have been avoided if more individuals had questioned their 'belonging' to a culture of short-term personal gain. A culture that suppresses free thinking, that requires absolute belonging to one way of being, only succeeds when the organisation does not have to change, when the outside world is static. But that's not our world. The speed of change in the external environment of any organisation means that cultures that stifle individual differences, individual innovation and perspectives that challenge the status quo are likely to lose out.

At a more local level, overidentification with one team, one section or one division can set up internal competition that undermines the success of the organisation's overall aim. A 'one-company' perspective is quite often on the checklist of competencies for promotion but the reality can be very much the opposite. Are you willing to give up your most effective staff member to help another team? Do you care what happens in Division B provided Division A, your division, hits its targets?

What about the other end of the extreme, where the level of loyalty is low, where there is a shared distrust or even disdain of the organisation's culture? Having a low level of loyalty is expensive. It's likely to go hand-in-hand with high staff turnover, freeing valuable employees to join the ranks of more attractive competitors. It leads to a fall in effort as employees place their sense of belonging elsewhere, maybe in their social life. Why slog your guts out for an organisation that you care little for when, for the same reward, you can do the basics and spend more time with your family or fishing? Where there is a low level of loyalty yet employees feel trapped by their circumstances and are unable to leave, subversive behaviour can occur where the sense of 'not belonging' is stronger than that of 'belonging'. Theft of physical things, theft of time or theft of confidential material can result. Whistle-blowers are, in the most part, people who have become so disillusioned with an organisation that they feel more affinity with those outside its boundaries than those within them.

The answer to the belonging question is balance. It's a dangerous policy to seek blind allegiance but to play no heed to creating loyalty risks an organisation having a short and turbulent life. All organisations have a culture of some kind. The key is not to allow it to evolve by accident or to keep to the old ways simply because it's just too tough to strive for change. The successful organisation of today actively seeks to build a culture that holds people together through a common purpose but allows for learning and challenge in the way that purpose is achieved, thus enabling the goals of individual employees to be nurtured. This is no easy task and it can't be achieved through old-style command and control management.

Belonging in a changing employment market

Careers today are more often made through a series of zig-zag moves between organisations than a steady rise within one. Add in periods of self-employment, redundancy, outsourcing or zero-hours contracts and it's to be expected that a sense of 'belonging' to any one organisation is transitory. A current trend to select 'outsiders' for vacant senior roles only serves to reinforce this. If I know that I must leave an organisation to progress, my attention will be split between my current job and the opportunities available externally, creating only a half-hearted sense of belonging.

In this world of organisation hopping, managers have limited time to build belonging before their most talented people pledge their allegiance elsewhere. Losing a small number of key players in a team can have a devastating effect on performance and the recovery process can be long and painful for those who remain, creating an unhealthy impact on their own sense of loyalty. Recruiting, inducting and developing new staff to the point at which they become fully functioning members of a team is frequently a lengthy and costly business. If you want to avoid this, attention must be given to the psychological contract of belonging.

How to damage belonging

By now, I hope you've received the message that it's easy to act against core needs inadvertently or intentionally. So, if you don't want to damage a sense of belonging, here are a few more things to avoid.

Keep changing the boundaries: A continually shifting agenda or frequent changes of leader, team members or even office space can all make it harder to build a sense of belonging. If your team is constantly changing, it will lose its shape and identity. Without an identity, there is nothing to belong to.

Make the belonging a one-way bargain: Belonging has costs and benefits for all parties involved. In a family, we both give and get support. If a team feels as though the effort is all one-way – meeting performance goals with little reward or acknowledgement for its members – don't expect loyalty. Similarly, if a manager's focus is overtly on his own interests (to get that promotion or bonus), he might think his staff belong to him but he won't be part of their gang.

Break the bonds that bind you by betraying trust: Few human beings are fools. They recognise organisational games. It doesn't matter what the manager promises; it's his actions that make an impact (the espoused versus the actual). By saying one thing then doing another, trust is lost, the rules of belonging are broken and loyalty marches firmly out of the door. Oh, and when it comes to betrayal, human beings have long, long memories.

Isolate people from each other: It's hard to feel we relate to others if our contact with them is limited. Even the most determined introvert needs some interaction. If lone time is not interspersed with contact time (from a simple coffee break with one other person to a team meeting with them all), we human beings tend to find other ways to make contact. Regrettably, our way may not be the most productive for work. In some organisations, wandering about just for some basic human contact can become a way of life. With the growing trend for staff to work at least part of their week at home, there is a risk that individuals begin to feel more connected with their home coffee machine and car radio than with their work colleagues.

Impose an identity: I have an aversion to company brochures that document an organisation's values or culture. I'm not too keen either on mass communication events that aim to tell people what they should do or believe. That's not to say that leaders shouldn't encourage their staff to think and behave in certain ways. My objection is when staff are told how to *feel*, and culture and values are very much about feeling. Initiatives of this kind come from the logical computer of the senior team, along the lines of 'If we write this, then it will be'. But human beings aren't so easily convinced. The heart is influenced by a range of needs, beliefs and circumstances. A company set of values is something I may read and agree with as an aspiration but whether I believe them, buy into them and belong to them is an entirely different matter.

By imposing an identity from on high, there is a greater risk of turning people off and thereby creating distance rather than switching on a sense of belonging. Think of a time when a new manager said to you, 'Why do you do that? In my last department, we did it like this so that's how I want it here.' Punches have been thrown for less.

How to strengthen belonging

I'm sure you already know what to do to strengthen belonging. Indeed, you may feel that the 'belonging' job is already done in your team. But belonging is an elusive creature. It can slip away silently without you noticing it's happening until your people start slipping away right after it. Here are a few reminders about how to build a sense of belonging that is likely to stick around.

Don't delay: Building belonging should be right up alongside your other top priorities. When new into a team, people decide quickly whether this is the place, or the leader, for them. That's why the quality of an induction process, or lack of one, can make a significant impact on new joiners. Don't be tempted to skip induction for new staff. Even if I swim rather than sink in a new role, I am unlikely to enjoy being pushed in and I will doubtless remember the unhelpful person who was responsible. If, as a manager, you are the newcomer, swift action is needed to signal the type of person and management style that your team can expect from you. Remember, you need to take a step towards your team as much as they need to step towards you.

Create a common purpose: Purpose doesn't have to be big, life-saving stuff. Manufacturing lids for bottles may not sound sexy but it's a critical part of our manufacturing industry. If purpose is clearly articulated and has some effect in the world, it's enough for people to decide whether they buy into it or not. Better still, a purpose that your team members create together and which has a personal connection for them is likely to engage both their hearts and computers. A fuzzy, distant or more generic purpose (like increasing profit for shareholders) or with a covert bias (like raising senior executive bonuses) is less likely to create loyalty, unless team members are on the receiving end of the dividend or bonus, of course. A shared purpose is a shared motivation to succeed. Having a purpose is a human being must-have; that's why Chapter 13 is devoted to this subject.

Create an identity shared by the members: Having decided where you are headed, define how you will work together to get there. Identity is not about specific objectives or targets; it's about the style and approach a team follows. Agree the 'stamp' of your team. What does your team want to be known for? Is it to do with quality, timeliness, creativity, good humour, all of these or something completely different? Agree explicit guidelines about how you'll work together for projects, meetings and so on. Be careful, though, not to set an identity in stone. Be sure to revisit it regularly. As team members change, it will need to be refreshed because, as noted earlier, identity cannot be imposed.

Build personal connections: People belong to common cultures, ambitions, professions, traditions and belief systems but most of all they belong to the people who share these attributes.

To build a sense of belonging, therefore, we have to create an environment where people get along at a personal level such that differences in style and personality can be accommodated. We don't have to be best buddies with colleagues to feel we are on the same side but do we need to find enough common ground to respect each other. If relationships are poor, something will give way. But don't be seduced by a quick-fix team-building approach here. There's only so much that Lego building, paintballing, horse whispering and trips to the bar can achieve in isolation. Building relationships requires trust and trust is a greedy thing; it needs to be fed and nurtured regularly if it is to grow. Hence, fostering respect, inclusion and communication in the everyday life of people at work is an ongoing project.

You may be thinking that this is a challenging task, and it can be. It's not within your gift as a manager to make people like each other but, like a theatre director, you can set the stage to make it more likely to happen. Role model the behaviour you expect to see in others, be explicit in your expectations of how team members should work together, keep watch to see how relationships are developing and help people to find common ground when they are struggling to do so by themselves. Yes, you already have enough to do without keeping everybody happy but good working relationships mean that team members belong to each other as well as to their manager and that's the oil that keeps the performance machine working.

Identify where you don't belong but retain respect: Strengthening belonging automatically strengthens not belonging. If you have human beings who have a high need for achievement, the belonging/not belonging divide can become competitive and, if unmanaged, healthy competition can quickly turn into disrespect, blame and then something decidedly unpleasant and unproductive. However, with guidance and a good example set by the manager, it's perfectly possible to enjoy, support and enthuse about one's own belonging without turning other groups into the enemy. When you celebrate your team's success, make it your business to congratulate other teams on their achievements too. Look for strands of common interest between groups so that, on some front at least, they stand together. By identifying where their sets overlap, you can create collaboration and a healthy spurring-on of performance. Deal with unhealthy competition and disrespect without compromise.

Walk the talk: The current buzzword in leadership development is 'authenticity'. An authentic leader is self-aware, open and truthful. If what you say is consistent with the way you behave, and consistent over time, your staff will grow to believe in you. Provided they like what they hear and see, they will belong to your approach and to your leadership. That means being willing to acknowledge when you don't know the way forward, when you make mistakes, when you have to apologise. It means allowing yourself to be seen as a human being. You may have been well-schooled in covering up your humanness behind your work clothes so being authentic might take something in the way of a psychological striptease. But, hey, that sounds more fun than being bundled up inside an unnecessary uniform that hides the most fascinating part of you.

What next?

Imagine that today everything in your life is perfect. Wow. Tomorrow, the conditions that made it all perfect are just the same. Another great day. Then the next day is the same and the next day is identical and the next day and the next day and the next day... yawn. What happened to perfect? Let's consider the need for change.

CHAPTER 11

I Change

Movement is part of the human condition. Physical movement keeps our bodies healthy. If we don't remain active, our muscles, bones and internal organs and the nerves that serve them begin to seize, rather like an engine left to rust in the rain. In today's jargon, we have to 'use it or lose it'. The need for movement and the change it creates are not just requirements of our physical selves. Psychologically, we need to *feel* we are in motion, not necessarily travelling down the highway or running a marathon but moving towards a goal.

Movement helps to define our boundaries as a person and our relationship with the world around us. When we create change, we stimulate feedback – our action creates a reaction. When we push, something shifts or pushes back. When we act, something happens. When we create, something is made. At a fundamental level, we know we exist because change has occurred.

Being stuck

When there seems little point in what we do because, despite the effort we make, 'everything' remains as it was, we're well and truly stuck. Everything? Surely, that's not possible. Just the fact that we're alive means something is on the move. Yes and no. The reason for the word 'everything' is that when we're stuck the intransigence of the one vital thing we want to shift is enough to overshadow other aspects of life that may well be changing. It becomes 'everything that matters' is stuck. If you've ever experienced a period in your life when you've been totally bored, living a routine you thought would never end, you will understand this.

The uneasy feeling of being stuck often creeps up on us. Over time, we may keep returning to an issue until, with enough repetition, it becomes constantly in our line of sight. Eventually, like a block in the road, this one issue becomes difficult to see around or beyond. Feeling trapped intellectually, emotionally or spiritually is a soulless feeling. It ranges from a mild haze to an all-consuming dark cloud. When there is no change, it's as if our identity begins to disintegrate. If we have no effect on the world, then who are we?

This sense of being stuck is highly individual. Undoubtedly, there are environmental conditions that make it more likely that we will feel rooted to the spot but how we react to an impasse varies. An economic recession puts the brakes on the plans of many. Careers can find themselves in a cul-de-sac due to technological change, a company takeover or government cuts. Life plans can be truncated by serious illness, disability or the death of a loved one. But difficult events don't always lead to feeling stuck. One man's depressing redundancy is another's liberation. In fact, the experience of dealing with adversity can be a life-affirming change even though the event that led to it caused pain. Perversely, the place we feel most stuck may, to others, appear to be a good place. It could even be somewhere we have deliberately chosen to be and worked hard to reach but, once arrived, we realise that the journey was more exciting than the destination itself. The adage 'too much of a good thing' can come true. What we once wanted can lose its shine through its endless sameness over time.

Unfortunately, the discomfort or sometimes panic induced by feeling stuck can lead to some disastrous decision-making because it's very easy to blame a sense of 'going nowhere' on the wrong someone or something when the true cause may lie elsewhere. Sometimes, the instigator of bad change may be our very own self if we aren't prepared to delve deep enough to understand what's really troubling us. To increase the chances of making change a positive experience, we must get to know in detail our desired direction of travel, even if we don't have a clue about our final destination.

I change and control

The reason being stuck is so debilitating is that it's the antithesis of hope. Hope is based on the belief that, even when times are bad, we can alter the course of our destiny, that we have some control over our future and that a better life may lie ahead. The importance of having an *internal locus of control*[38] and a sense of *self-efficacy*[39] has been documented by numerous psychologists but you probably don't need to delve into their research papers to know this to be true. If you have ever felt as though you cannot change the course of your life no matter what you do, you will be aware how dark and hopeless this feels. Human beings need hope to survive.

The concept of hope embraces the notion that a positive outcome lies ahead; we do not hope for change that is harmful or unpleasant. So, although human beings need movement, it doesn't mean that all change is regarded as good. Clearly, acquiring a life-threatening illness is not a positive way out of a boring job. Marrying the person of your dreams who turns out to be the source of your nightmares is unlikely to be good either. A series of disasters does not feel like change, more the sameness of bad luck.

The key point about movement and change is that the direction in which we move needs to be of our choosing or, if it wasn't our own choice, it must be change that we can accept. If it's change that we can take an active part in shaping, then better still. Change over which I have some control, and which is flowing in a direction of my choosing, is uplifting.

Recent research in the field of positive psychology has shown how hope and optimism can impact on our emotional and physical well-being.[40] It affects the coping strategies we adopt when faced with illness or emotional distress which in turn alters longer-term outcomes. In a world where the cost of health care is soaring and life expectancy is increasing, interventions that help people develop a more positive outlook are already beginning to show promising results.[41]

Martin Seligman, the psychologist who identified how animals and people acquire a general *learned helplessness* when they realise they cannot change their destiny, has shown that the reverse can be true also. We can increase our level of happiness, particularly when we identify what we are good at (our signature strengths) and use these abilities in a new way.[42] That's the power of I change.

Moving with age

Anyone in, or beyond, their middle years will appreciate how our need for change alters with time. Most young children can't wait to grow up. I remember when, as the youngest of three children, I wasn't tall enough to go to the swimming pool with my siblings. In my head, I created an extraordinary vision of the swimming baths as a swirling, bottomless sea. When I was finally deemed tall enough to stand in the shallow end without drowning, I was very disappointed. The pool seemed so safe in comparison to my imagined ocean. When we are very small, we see the opportunities available to older children and adults and feel aggrieved that they are out of our reach. Then, with the passage of time and increasing effort, we arrive at a 'gateway', the age at which we too can take part in climbing the ladder of a slide, going to nursery, swimming in the big pool, going to school, attending the disco, learning to drive, voting and so on. Sadly, as with the swimming pool, our satisfaction at this arrival is often short-lived because, parading right before our eyes, is an array of yet more things in which we are still not old enough or skilled enough to take part. Then off we go again, heading for another desired destination.

In growing up, there are many gateways through which to pass. In our early life, it can feel as though change is laid out before us as a never-ending conveyor belt, with families and schools formalising our passage by fixed timelines and measures of our progress. As we pass through our teens, college years and on into work, other life goals provide a path to follow – relationships, careers, building a home of our own, building a family. There is so much to move towards, we rarely need to consider what all this change means to us. It's just part of everyday life until, at some point, the pace of change begins to slow. Choices that earlier in life felt like an ever-increasing set of roads to travel begin to reduce into fixed highways as the decisions of the past dictate today's options. What we want, and what is possible by virtue of our abilities or by circumstance, may no longer go hand-in-hand. Sometimes, it may feel as though someone has flicked the 'moving forwards' switch to 'going backwards'.

If this sounds depressing, it shouldn't. Certainly, once we are past the flurry of our early years, movement is not provided to us as a given but, if we choose to give it the attention it deserves, we can be the engineers of our change. We can choose our goals and define our journey. Rather than being swept along in an unthinking way, we can make more informed and considered decisions based on our experience and our knowledge. With age, we recognise that change is as much about how we think, what we value and what we believe, as it is about what we do. For many older people, developing wisdom is a goal well worth striving for.

Although the type of change on offer to us alters with time, yielding losses as well as gains, our need for movement does not diminish. The challenge is to keep reframing our goals and selecting new destinations so that we are still moving forward, whatever our stage of life.

What's this got to do with work?

We can't expect work to be a constant source of excitement. Most roles have elements that are tedious, boring or repetitive interspersed with elements that are stimulating, rewarding and maybe even fun. But, if the overall balance is towards the tedious end, the long-term outlook won't be pretty. The need for change is present in us all but the pace at which we want to stride forward varies considerably. The eager beaver, who relishes the buzz of risk and speed, may create problems by trying to rush ahead without the skills or groundwork needed to allow change to succeed. The cautious perfectionist, who needs to inspect every step of the journey with care, may hold others back. The manager's challenge is to work with each individual to identify the trajectory they want to follow and then to consider this path against what the organisation has to offer. Staying still should be an option only in specific circumstances, typically when the change taking place outside work is absorbing so much emotional energy that there is no stamina left for further change within work (for example, during a period of ill health or a family crisis or where learning is taking place elsewhere, such as completing an Open University degree).

It may take some time before an individual realises they are stuck but, when they do, the cost can be high. As the momentum for movement is difficult to repress for long, when we can't move the way we want, we wriggle about until we find a different direction in which to put our efforts. This new path may not be in harmony with the goals of the organisation. It might result in an individual retreating inwards, withdrawing their effort and enthusiasm from their role. Or it might lead them to project their frustration and disillusionment right into the centre of their work. Hence, a strong sense of being stuck can directly or indirectly disrupt progress. It interferes not only with the individual but with the lives of those around him. It has the potential to create a negative rumble that shakes its way through teams and departments and, in some instances, be carried beyond the walls of the organisation to those outside (to customers, clients, potential customers, potential staff, the media). The impact of this rumble can command a high price. Leaving people feeling stuck costs money through disruption, loss of reputation and loss of talented people.

How to diminish 'I change'

Even if we don't set out to keep people in one place, it's quite easy to do so through the types of managerial actions given below.

Design unstimulating jobs: Give bright people repetitive but difficult jobs with little prospect of development and, before you know it, they see imaginary fences all around them. No wonder the turnover at many call centres is high. And let's not restrict our thinking to graduates and highly skilled people here. Why should nursing auxiliaries, care-workers, cleaners, fast-food workers, warehouse staff etc. be expected to repeat the same tasks relentlessly with no sense of movement? They have potential waiting to be tapped and their needs as human beings are just the same.

Behave like a parent: Keeping a tight control over decision-making may seem like a sound way of reducing risk but it's also a quick way to create a disempowered and demotivated team. Individuals who feel the direction of change is always decided elsewhere by a managerial 'mum' or 'dad' are likely to respond like children, either creating disruptive change or becoming highly dependent. If your staff tell you that you don't delegate enough (and that's decision-making as well as tasks), then they're probably right. Why are you hanging onto control if others are ready and capable of defining and creating change?

Leave potential untapped: Perhaps one of the greatest tragedies of the recent economic depression is the high level of young people unable to find satisfying jobs. Coinciding as it does with the highest levels of people attending university, we now have a population of young adults with strong aspirations who cannot find work and, consequently, are at greater risk of mental health issues.[43] This is not just a problem for the individuals concerned; it's a problem for society as whole. To have a generation scarred by lack of fulfilment is a worrying state of affairs. Yet, lack of jobs is only one reason that potential goes untapped. Biased thinking about recruitment means that those with talent can often be overlooked. A case in point is that of able individuals who have taken a break to have their children or look after their ageing parents. People do not suddenly lose their ability to think and learn just because they've been at home for a few years. Organisations can also become fixed in their thinking about the qualifications and experience needed to do a job well. Do good nurses really need a degree? Do managers in the public sector really need a master's-level qualification to take a senior role? Does an oil company really need graduates with first-class degrees only? The research to support these selection criteria is often lacking and, even if it does exist, it's impossible to predict what will ultimately lead to success in a rapidly changing world – as noted earlier, yesterday's significant correlation may say little about tomorrow's needs. Another bias, particularly for senior level roles, is the tendency to look for ready-built candidates rather than those who have potential to grow into a role. Have you noticed how many senior people seem to move from one organisation to another simply because they have a similar role on their CV, even if their performance in it was decidedly poor? We need to be more adept at looking for potential talent and the ability to learn, not existing knowledge (which can, by and large, be acquired quickly by able people). Leaving potential untapped leaves people with potential stuck.

Put the wrong person in the wrong job: Another way to waste potential is to mismatch a person with a job. When we're in the wrong role, we tend to know it, which makes performing well, keeping motivated and developing skills a tough challenge. Bad selection decisions are made for many reasons but they often relate to taking a fragmented view of an individual rather than considering the whole human being.

Strip out the opportunity for change: Making processes more efficient may save money but it can also diminish challenge and reduce the scope for growth. We are familiar with this concept on the assembly lines of manufacturing but managerial roles can also be stripped of interest. The practice of centralising or outsourcing functions like procurement, recruitment and HR can limit the sense of control a manager has over his job. The introduction of sophisticated technology may mean that the intellectual component of a role is diminished, leaving the human being as the minder of a machine or computer. Growing regulation can lead to restrictions in how a job is performed, reducing the scope for an individual's judgement. Death by meetings and paperwork overload can lead to a deep sense of boredom. 'Rust out', a wonderfully evocative term coined in the 1980s for being stuck, should concern today's leaders as much as its overdrive cousin, 'burn out'.[44]

Ignore the need for development: A golden rule for a good manager is to help his staff develop, preferably matching each individual's goals with those of the organisation. But what if the development opportunities on offer are in short supply and the skills needed to assist people to develop are equally thin on the ground? Then it's easier for the manager to whizz through the development section of appraisal, perhaps grabbing the first training programme that comes to mind, or leave the section blank for the employee to fill in later, if it doesn't cost too much, of course. If this sounds like your world, be wary. Because human beings need change, they will still develop one way or another even if their manager pays little heed to development. What they develop, however, may not be to their manager's liking and, even if it is, the growth it yields may not be enough to keep them committed to their role.

Assume another's desired direction of travel is the same as yours: So, you want a fast-moving career, rising through the ranks at speed with a megabucks salary and endless travel? You may be surprised that I don't. One person's work heaven is quite different to another's, so don't blame me if I don't respond to the management style that suits you.

Assume that people stay the same: What was top of my agenda for change last year may have been overtaken by another need. What I want and what I don't want shifts with time, experience and the environment. Because Mr Smith in accounts has always seemed to want a quiet life doesn't mean he wants one now. Our appetite for change varies.

How to strengthen 'I change'

Entire businesses exist with the sole purpose of educating others in the intricacies of organisational change to the point that 'change management', where the direction of change is more or less imposed, is now part of the everyday lexicon of business. Despite this, we are still insufficiently appreciative of change as a fundamental part of each person's make-up, i.e. when the direction of change is driven by the individual. Try the following if you want to address this shortfall.

Invest time in exploring what change is needed: Sometimes we don't know what we want, just that we haven't got it. Coaching an individual to explore what they need to be motivated at work is time well spent. To be an effective coach, you will need to keep your assumptions about the person in front of you in check, be honest about their performance, help them shape a plan through good listening and offer suggestions for change – don't just be a sponge. However, try not to expect revolutionary change. Remember that movement doesn't have to be monumental to refresh us and keep us happy. And, if you have people who agree to development goals but never seem to meet them, go back to the beginning and explore why this is happening. Don't accept excuses without understanding what lies beneath them. Patterns that repeat themselves usually indicate that there's something else going on to keep your people stuck. Help them to identify the 'glue' that's responsible.

Encourage individuals to accept their power to create change: By approaching others in an adult-to-adult manner, you set the expectation that they have the power to determine their own future. Be careful not to create or accept dependency. Push back when someone wants you to take responsibility for their future. Encourage and support others to develop a sense of independent thought even if you don't share their perspective.

Use your team to create movement: If you are the person who always sets the direction for your team, you can be assured that there will be times when people don't want to follow you. That's just the way it is. Instead, allow your people the opportunity to build a direction with you. Use their ideas. Create a buzz about the road you are travelling together even if the rest of the organisation is distinctly buzz-less. On a day-to-day basis, hand over power where possible. Delegate, loosen your grip and take calculated risks on people so they can experiment with new areas.

Identify everyone's (yes, everyone's) talents: Conduct an audit of the skills possessed by the people in your team. Make it broad-reaching (what people do outside as well as in work that indicates potential). Add to this their interests – what they would like to do if the opportunity came along. If they're not sure what to aim for, arrange for individuals to experience a 'taster' by sitting alongside others in different roles or allow them to 'try out' certain tasks. Give them something tangible to work towards.

Be creative with development: Development doesn't have to be expensive in terms of cash but it does need time. You may have to allow someone to go 'off-piste' to achieve their goals but if that strengthens their performance in the long run it will be worth it. Look beyond the organisation's training brochure. Consider how team members can learn from each other and from you. Recognise that development is more than learning skills and acquiring knowledge; it's about how we think and feel. Draw in people from other departments, businesses and places to help stretch the thinking of your team even if the focus of their work is radically different to your own. Surprise your people with what can be learned from simple actions. Encourage team members to reflect regularly on what they're learning from their roles. If the answer is not much, then their roles need enriching.

Deal with performance issues: If performance is stuck or going backwards, tackle it without delay. Try to resist using your loud voice or a bold typeface to demand what you've already demanded before. Your role is to help the individual become 'unstuck' so that they can move past what was holding them. Good glue-removing options are listening (human being detective skills are vital here), reshaping the role, adding extra support or resources, providing development or arranging an exit strategy from your team.

When becalmed, fill sails with other change: When, for whatever reason, morale is low and the team feels stuck, don't ignore it, explore it. You may be moving along happily but your people may feel very stuck indeed. If this happens, investigate the cause and do what you can to help people stay temporarily anchored (so they don't feel they are slipping backwards at least), hold out hope for change, and press for movement on other fronts so the anchor can be raised. Whatever you do, don't keep pursuing a hopeless cause. What's dead is best thrown overboard to allow you to sail on elsewhere.

Challenge existing recruitment/selection processes that keep people stuck: If you use blanket screening methods, check the validity on which they are based. Where is the evidence that they work? Do research on how your selection procedures screen out talent as well as screen it in (where do people you turned down end up?). After all, Thomas Edison's teachers told him he was too stupid to learn anything. Walt Disney was fired from a newspaper because he lacked imagination and a certain firm I used to work for declined to take on a very young Richard Branson as a client because he looked too unreliable. Everyone has potential but it can be heavily disguised. Finding the role that matches that potential is the magic key to performance because it maximises both skill and motivation. Look around your organisation. Can you see people who have untapped talent? Maybe the person on reception could be a fabulous client handler. Maybe the graduate stacking shelves at night is a skilled graphic designer. Maybe the administrative assistant knows more about the role he administers than you realise. And why not challenge your own selection biases? What 'mould' do you expect people to fit and what are the consequences of this? Hint: they won't all be positive.

Recognise that movement does not have to be in work: Remember that, for some, there are stages in life when change at work is just not wanted because the need for change is being met elsewhere. When my children were very young, the change and challenge in my home life allowed me to accept a higher level of stability in my work life. Now that my children are grown, my hunger for a sense of progression at work has returned, although my desired direction has undoubtedly shifted.

Be prepared to let go: When someone is revving up to move off, it takes considerable energy to keep your foot on the brake to hold them still. Sometimes it's better to help them on their way. And you'd better be nice about it. You never know, they could end up as your client or boss one day.

What next?

A good human being detective can derive much information from pure observation but observation alone absorbs a considerable amount of time and dedication. Now, I suspect that you have so many other pressing tasks on your to-do list that observation might end up being relegated to the bottom of your agenda. A simpler, and more realistic, way to get the data you need is to take the direct route. Just ask for it! However, this is two-sided affair. To get meaningful answers, we may first need to help people find their voice.

CHAPTER 12

Helping Human Beings to Find a Voice

B eing heard is central to all core needs. If we are not heard, we are left powerless. How can we feel secure, know that we matter, that we belong or that we have some control over the direction in which our lives travel if our voice, our thoughts, our beliefs are heard by no one other than ourselves? Being heard means having efficacy, influence, a say on the world, whether that's on the small stage of our immediate environment or on the bigger platform of a business, public body, union, political party or scout group.

To be heard, human beings have first to believe that we have a voice that's worth listening to, that we have a right to be heard. This isn't as straightforward as it seems. Many of us are nervous to speak up, literally as well as figuratively. We are cowed by the sound of others' ideas. Their voice seems in some way superior, more articulate or smarter than our own. At the other end of the spectrum, there are those who feel a pressure to fill any silence with the sound of their ideas, leaving little space to hear anything other than their own voice. Interestingly, this ongoing voice may not be audible so that there is the appearance of listening but the voice is still gabbling away inside, filling the space just the same. There is a fear in this type of voice – what value have I, if I have nothing to say or do not know what is best?

True communication isn't a one-way street. To know that we are heard we require feedback. A response, even if that response is silence, gives us information that helps us decide if, and how, to move forward. Of course, communication doesn't go in a single line. It's a series of loops and exchanges. Watching skilful communicators is like watching the ebb and flow of the sea on a beach. The water flows in different ways, from a gracious glide to a pounding roar according to prevailing conditions. As these conditions change, so the power of the water responds, altering the amount of ground the sea covers on each flow. In a similar way, a good communicator is sensitive to the environment and adjusts the content and style of communication to make sure messages have the best chance of reaching their intended destination.

The flow is only half of the sea's movement. The ebb is the equal and opposite force needed to keep the sea moving. In the ebb, the tide pulls the water back, leaving space for the sand. And what happens? From the exposed beach, hidden crustaceans, worms and other slimy things pop up unexpectedly. Seaweed loses its shape and falls to the ground. The sand, pebbles and shells seem to rush after the water, following its course. When the flow is silent, when we are silent and leave space, things we had not heard or seen before can come to light. What looked to be one thing may appear as something different.

Good communicators pay as much attention to the ebb as to the flow. They make space for other people so that they can be heard. They influence people both through their message and their willingness to hear. What's more, they manage this ebb and flow of communication not by slick technique, smooth patter, a therapist's training or being two degrees smarter than the other person. Instead, they apply liberal doses of two simple but relatively rare attributes (and here's the R word again): respect and curiosity.

Respect

To respect another is not necessarily to like what they do. We can disagree profoundly with another's views but accept their right to hold them. This is the principle of a democratic and free society. When this principle is lacking, human beings become polarised according to power, wealth, tribe, religion, political party or any manner of damaging divides in which one side is a winner and the other is a loser. Without respect, we stop seeing other people as fellow human beings. Our history books and present-day newspapers are filled with examples of the bloody consequences of this catastrophic error.

Who then deserves respect? As noted previously, we are all afforded respect by virtue of being born as equal human beings. However, this is only our starting point. We build additional respect based on our actions, by how we live our lives. Does this mean that some human beings become more or less worthy than others? Yes and no. While we may admire people for their position in a hierarchy or for their knowledge and experience, these attributes alone don't command additional respect. It's how we use what we have that creates respect, whether our role is complex or simple, senior or junior. Respect comes from action because to get respect you have also to give it.

There is only one circumstance when our entitlement to respect is diminished, taking us back to the respect starting block, so to speak. If we abuse others, we forfeit much of the respect we have built. We don't lose the fundamental respect of our shared human nature (even a murderer is entitled to a fair trial) but that's where the line is drawn. Hence, abusers never control through respect. They rule by fear and circumstance alone and, should the circumstances change, their authority is short-lived.

Respect doesn't stand alone. It's a relative thing. It's about me and you. The respect I give you depends first on the respect I afford to myself, whether I see myself as:

- *less important:* you're better than me; you deserve more respect than me,

- *more important:* I'm better than you; you deserve less respect than me,

- *equal to the other:* both of us have equal value.

How we position ourselves in this way has significant implications for the degree of comfort we feel in voicing our views and in listening to others.

I am less important than you: Never doubt the power of self-belief. Technical brilliance, expert knowledge and years of experience count for nothing if we doubt our own value. If we lack self-belief, we put ourselves at the bottom of a steep hill before even reaching the starting line and it can be a long climb up. How are we to make our voice heard if we don't believe anyone would be interested in our views? How can we be trusted by others if we don't trust ourselves? Human beings are very adept at spotting those who are unsure of their own merit. We seem to have an internal detector that picks it up. Even if we can't put a finger on exactly what the issue is, we know something isn't right.

All human beings have self-doubts but some doubts are more damaging than others. When these doubts encroach on our fundamental sense of value, then we put ourselves at risk of becoming a victim. That doesn't mean we choose to be a victim but that we may accept a higher level of abuse because we feel powerless to change the situation or to defend ourselves. We may even come to believe the abuser's message – you are less worthy than I, therefore my needs prevail.

To be heard and to have influence, it's essential to keep the notion of equality of value firmly in mind and to challenge disrespect (respectfully!). Those who come from the 'less-important' perspective must become comfortable with the skill of assertion. Our everyday use of language often confuses the term aggression and assertion. *Aggression* involves losing respect for the other. *Assertion* means respecting one's own position and believing in the right to express it, without hostility, even if you have to repeat it over and over again. Assertion is about belief and will. It represents the acceptance of our equal right to be heard.

I am more important than you: There is sad truth that human beings are easily seduced by their own advertising. If enough people tell us that we are terrific, perhaps even more terrific than others, then we tend to believe them. This may in fact be true in terms of our capabilities but it doesn't mean that we're better human beings. In a hierarchical organisation, it's easy for those holding power to forget this. Indeed, some organisational cultures appear to deliberately foster disrespectful behaviour where leaders and managers seem to believe it's their duty to be unpleasant. This *organisational abuse* is not rare. It's alive and well and breeding happily on the role models of those who haven't learned a better way of operating. But it's growing on shaky ground. Power executed through disrespect may look hardy but it's weak. Its existence relies on a limited number of circumstances. Cultures where abusive disrespect is common are unlikely to thrive unless employees are tied in by high salaries, have nowhere else to go or have become so immune to abuse that they may both receive and inflict it on others.

The sense of being above others is what converts influence into manipulation. While the skills needed for both are identical, they differ profoundly in their *intention*, what we carry in our heart at the outset. Manipulation is seen at an individual level (the unscrupulous salesman, the offer too good to be true, the 'bribe' of a better job that never materialises, the quiet, threatening word of warning) but it's also seen on a grander scale. When customers are treated as fools who will buy products that aren't worth the money, that's organisational manipulation. When, in an effort to make them stay, staff are not told the truth about the shaky financial performance of a business until it goes under, that's manipulation. When employees are informed that they are not allowed to whistle-blow because it will affect profit or media coverage, that's manipulation too.

If you think that this sort of thing never happens in your organisation, think again. Abuse and manipulation arise from poor leadership and poor management. Feeling 'one up' on others is a very human thing to feel and it's you and me as well as our leaders and managers that feel it, although, I hope, on a minor scale. So, what's to be done? The first step is to make it acceptable to 'call it' when disrespect happens. When the consultant speaks to a junior doctor or a nurse with contempt in his voice, it should be ok to point this out. When a senior manager repeatedly cancels meetings with his team because he has better things to do, it should be ok to tell him that this is disrespectful. When unfavourable feedback from staff surveys is ignored, it should be accepted that staff can ask for the feedback to be revisited. The second step is to recognise and reward behaviour that marries both respect and performance. Managers who deliver without recourse to bullying, rudeness or disrespect should be publicly acknowledged for their achievement. Staff can only be heard, and feel heard, where openness and respect exist and a culture of acceptable challenge is fostered.

I am equal to you: When we give due recognition and respect for the achievements of others but hold ourselves equal as human beings, we free our voice. By turfing out the emotional clutter that holds us back and acknowledging our right to be heard, we gain a better control over our emotions and ward off any potential ambush by shyness or aggression. Don't think this gives us licence to behave like an annoying schoolchild, however, constantly shouting out in class without having the answers. No. It simply means that, where appropriate, we accept that our views matter and, because we believe it, we are more likely to command attention, have impact and be heard.

Curiosity

To be curious means to have both the desire and the patience to understand our own and others' thinking. The desire aspect springs from a recognition that humans are highly complex beings. To the curious individual, unpicking what humans do is endlessly fascinating. The patience component is found in real listening, not the fake listening of learned head nodding or a tutored 'ah ha' while not having the slightest concern for what the other human being is communicating. Curiosity doesn't accept pat, obvious solutions. It always expects there to be more than what's seen or heard at a surface level and it's never satisfied that we fully understand ourselves. Being curious means really wanting to know, not merely asking because that's what the system tells us to do.

As a manager, your role is to facilitate the performance of your team and being curious is crucial to this endeavour. Firstly, your curiosity must span what others think and feel about themselves so that you truly get to know your people as human beings. Then, your desire to know, your nosiness if you like, must keep nagging you to investigate their perspective on the problems that fall into your management in-basket. If you are not curious, you take the burden of solving these problems on your own shoulders, and that can be a heavy and uncomfortable load. While being regarded as the source of all solutions may give you a warm, heroic glow inside, it rarely leads to the best outcome for the team or the organisation. What happens when you fall under, or get on, that metaphorical bus? The capability of your team will have been stunted by their dependency on you. And why should your solutions be the best, anyway? The people on the ground often have information and ideas that are closer to the pragmatic reality of a situation than a manager one step away. How often have you heard staff say, 'we could have told you that' at the end of an expensive intervention by an external consultant? A major part of a manager's job is to have the curiosity to facilitate communication, facilitate ideas and to listen. If this means giving up your status as the hero, then so be it. If you give others space to use their voices and to share responsibility, you will rise in their roll call of respect and generate solutions that stick.

How to help others to find a voice

The terms respect and curiosity are heart-warming aspirations and few would deny their importance. Translating such aspirations into pragmatic behaviour to enable others to find their voice is another matter. To get serious about respect and curiosity, we have to start demanding it and rewarding good practice when we see it. Consider your own management style against the following 'to-dos'.

Make space to hear: To help the people you manage find a voice, you must first consider whether the style *you* adopt allows them to be heard. Challenge yourself on the following questions and be truthful because there's no point in trying to fool yourself. Really, there isn't.

- Do you create opportunities for your staff to contribute – both in terms of your time and by giving signals that you're curious about what they have to say?

- Do you really listen when they speak? That means not cutting them off, building on what they say and truly considering their ideas. Or do you ride over their contribution and move straight on to your own views?

- Do you invite those who are naturally quiet to contribute or do you assume that not speaking up means they have nothing in their head?

- How creative have you allowed your people to be? Do you encourage them to take you on a different course than the direction you have charted?

- Can you recall ignoring the concerns of your people only for them to come to pass at a later date?

- When it comes to it, do you really care what your people say or are your efforts merely window dressing? You may hold your hands up in horror at this point and cry 'of course I care' but if I asked your team would they say that you valued their views?

- How many of their, versus your, ideas have you put into action in the last year?

You can measure these behaviours to get a clearer sense of what you do against what you think you do. If you really want to know how much space you create, make a recording of a team meeting and then ask someone to make a simple tally of who filled the greatest part of the airtime. Break the conversation down into who asks questions, who answers questions, who puts in ideas – whatever you want to know – to find out what's really going on. You will be surprised by the results. If you do most of the talking in team meetings, you need to change.

On a similar note, how much space do you afford clients and customers to express their views and, when they do, how much notice do you take?

- Are you giving clients/customers what you *have* rather than what they *want/need*?

- Does it feel easier not to listen in order to avoid the hassle of changing things?

- Are the views of service users regarded as an obstacle or a springboard for creative thinking?

- Is collecting views an end in itself or does it produce real change?

- Are client/customer/service users respected as human beings or as objects to be dealt with?

Check your assumptions: Filters formed in our heart or computer lead to helpful shortcuts in understanding others (e.g. people from that department always need this kind of information to make a decision; Mr X will only accept suggestions from his team, so plant the idea there first). Alas, they can also lead us astray because our filters sneakily encourage us to assume that others think and feel as we do, to believe what rocks our boat will rock theirs too. This creates internal 'noise' that can make it difficult to hear another's voice accurately. It's difficult to understand another's view of the world if we keep translating it into our own. When we say, 'I know just what you mean/ how you feel', it's unlikely to be true. The simple answer to this problem is to check out if your understanding is correct. When you're listening, don't just write notes and assume you've got the right end of the stick. Take the time to go back and clarify. A simple 'Can I just check if I've understood this correctly...' is often enough. Haste is the enemy of accurate listening and patience is, indeed, an extremely rewarding virtue. It's better to slow down or choose a better time to talk than to spare only a few brief moments and hear a sketchy or inaccurate account of the true message. When we're in a hurry, we're more likely to draw on our assumptions to speed up the process.

Don't double-task when you're listening, just listen: When you're listening, how often do you find yourself thinking of your reply while the speaker is still talking? If you're not sure, answer the following questions.

- Do you jump in with your contribution quickly after the other person has spoken without thinking much about what they said last?

- Are your responses sometimes unrelated to the key points raised but follow the agenda you walked in with? Think politician here and you'll know what I mean.

- Do you finish off the other person's sentence?

- Do you realise, later in a conversation, that you can't remember what has been said earlier in the same discussion?

If you answered yes to any of the above, then you are probably guilty of attempting the impossible – getting the most out of two thinking processes at once. However smart we have become on the evolutionary tree of cleverness, we human beings are not great at thinking two things at once. We can certainly 'get by' doing this but, when it comes to quality, the more tasks we take on, the more quality we lose. The tasks of 'listening to what is being said' and 'thinking of our next reply' interfere with each other. We can't do both justice at the same time.

So why do we try to do it? Typical reasons are fear of embarrassment (what if I have nothing to say when he stops talking?), the desire to look clever (I'm supposed to look smart here so I had better think of something smart to say), habit (I've always done it that way) and an inability to turn off our inner voice (if I'm not thinking, then what will I do?). Fear of embarrassment and the desire to look clever are the flip side of the same thing. In both instances, there is a fear of looking a fool. Maybe at school we learned that we had to have an answer ready for the teacher or maybe we felt less able because other children got in before us. Maybe at work (or in a marriage) the prevailing culture is to have a pre-prepared agenda and thus people never listen to each other in the moment. Concern that there will be a vacuum if we temporarily turn off our thinking is a misunderstanding. *Turning off* does not mean doing nothing. It means *turning on* to the other person. By stilling our inner language, we can really hear what's happening.

Whatever the reason for our poor listening, we can improve it if we have more trust in our own ability. Our brains work very quickly (hangover mornings excepted). If you listen to the end of another person's sentence without formulating your reply at the same time, paradoxically it will be easier to find the right reply because you will be on target, having focused on the other person's ideas. If you do need extra time to think, it's likely to be so short that it won't be noticeable. If, on the odd occasion it is, it will be regarded as a positive sign of interest. I urge you to experiment with this. Deliberately try not to formulate a reply while another person is speaking. See what happens.

Brush up your skills as a human being detective: Revisit the ideas given in Chapter 3 about listening to the whole person. Develop your skills in active listening but don't get overly concerned about technique; it comes a long way behind getting your attitude right in terms of helping others find a voice. Human beings hear sincerity, curiosity and respect before they hear question structure. A lousy question coming from the right place will be far more effective than a perfectly constructed question smothered by lack of interest.

Coach: Simply telling people to *speak up* is unlikely to work where there is a pattern of reticence around expressing views. If individuals are finding it difficult to give voice to their ideas despite being given opportunities and encouragement for their contribution, you will need to help them identify and unstick the glue holding them put. So, put on your coaching hat, refresh your coaching skills, agree small goals and give positive feedback for success, discretely, to help in the process of developing confidence. You will need a good dose of curiosity and patience to make coaching successful. And don't expect a transformation overnight as patterns that have been in place for many years can be very sticky indeed. Most importantly, don't give up. Some people are quieter than others but their input, when it eventually comes, can have the value of gold because it has been well thought through.

How to find your own voice

Many managers are comfortable communicators within their own team but find their confidence drains away in unfamiliar situations or with more forceful personalities/senior players. If that's you, here are a few tips to bear in mind and to pass on to others when coaching.

Believe in what you say: Honesty is definitely the best policy. Most human beings are good at sniffing out suspicious communication and, at some point, untruths are likely to be exposed. There are few people who can sound convincing giving the party line if they don't agree with it or if they know it to be untrue. To come across as a person with conviction, you must have it. Aim to be as frank and honest as you can be. If you are being pressured to massage the truth, say little or be prepared to accept the consequences.

Prepare your thinking: Before walking into a challenging situation, stop and consider your own internal communication system – what messages are you telling 'you'? What's going on in your head? Are you putting yourself down? Are you putting the client/colleague/staff member down? Are you reminding yourself of the times when similar situations have gone wrong? If your head isn't in the right place before you enter a difficult situation, your negative internal voice will lead you into trouble. Instead, take another stroll around the block, send the lift down to the ground floor again, offer to get coffee for everyone, or do whatever you can to get the small amount of time needed to give yourself a good talking to – and make it positive. If you think you lack in skills and experience, remind yourself that you are still equal in the human being stakes. If the people you are meeting can be bullying, tell yourself you have a right to be heard and to be assertive. Remind yourself of your successes and that you wouldn't be there unless there was good reason for it. And, if you are the senior person and feel the pressure of always having to come up with the right answer, tell yourself that you are equally valuable without doing this. Your value as a human being does not depend on it.

See human beings as human beings: If you are struggling with feeling equal to more senior, or bigger, louder, scarier people, try thinking about them away from the work situation. However important they are, in the rest of life they will be just like us. They will probably have a partner with whom they fall out from time to time. They may have health worries, have put on weight, be scared of spiders, have socks with holes, have a difficult mother-in-law, have a difficult boss, have children who are a handful, have toothache etc. All people have ordinary human being issues to deal with, just like us. Whatever their list of agonies, they will succeed or make a mess of them, just like us. If you're finding it hard to believe this, imagine the person who is making you feel anxious in a more human situation. I've always found visualising an important person in pyjamas buttoned up to the neck, complete with woolly, check dressing gown and hot water bottle, reduces even the most pompous individual to an equal. A word of warning. Your aim should be to take away your fear, not to degrade others so be careful not to verge on the disrespectful side with your imaginary creations.

Don't put up with bullies: Bullies have a need to prove their superiority to feel good about themselves, otherwise, there would be no need to bully. There is something missing in the bully that makes them feel inadequate and fragile. Most bullies are blind to this but it doesn't change the reality that those who try so hard to prove their strength are often the most fragile underneath. It can be strangely comforting to remember that the people who make our life most difficult are often the most troubled, even if they haven't realised it yet! Interestingly, although challenging a bully can be a frightening affair, it often leads to a positive change in their behaviour and greater respect for the challenger. Sometimes the bully is waiting for someone to push back and stop him. If this is too threatening to do alone, look for allies to back you up or, rather than confront the individual yourself, report the bullying behaviour to someone who is able to take action. Above all, don't suffer in silence.

Try not to respond out of anger: When our heart is in overdrive, our computer is on hold. Hence, if someone annoys or frustrates us to the point of anger, we're not in the best position to respond in a productive way. It's easy to be provoked and meet aggression with aggression but it rarely takes the situation forward unless, of course, we are in fear of our own safety. Assertion not aggression is the most powerful way of conveying a message and we can't act assertively unless we are in control of our thinking and feeling combined. If you feel your anger rising, it's far better to take a deep breath or to walk away until the surge of emotion has subsided, your computer is back in action and you can act assertively. Hot anger rarely wins the case, even if the case is justified.

Use logical persuasion at the right time: We learn logical persuasion from an early age at school and, as such, it becomes a powerful, inbuilt programme for our internal 'computer'. Unemotional, based on facts and vital to making sense of our world, we use this type of logic to lay out the framework of our ideas with data to support it. Having got the gist of our thinking, other people can then add to or adjust it and, all things being well, help build a more useful picture of the world. The downside of our familiarity with logical persuasion is that we often use it in a knee-jerk manner, making it our first choice for most occasions. By so doing, we can easily miss the significance of deeper matters of the 'heart'. The consequence of this favouritism is that we can become caught up in apparently logical arguments about a surface issue without first considering the problem that may underlie it (the pseudo-logic raised in Chapter 2). Consider a difficult issue that keeps being raised at work. You have the answer but no one seems to hear it. Facts, evidence and sound argument don't seem to solve it. What deeper problem could this be masking? Who is avoiding the underlying issue? You may need to steel yourself to bring this to the surface but it will save time and probably make you less frustrated in the long run if you do. You will not be heard on one issue if another is blocking its path.

Make communication a 'performance': You can't expect to be heard if you are crushingly dull or monotonous. Human beings tolerate tedium for a short while but most will switch off when faced with a delivery that is too quiet, too long, too over-the-top, too fast, too slow, too complex (think weather forecast) or too much of the same thing. For the ear, eye and brain to stay engaged, they need variety. Whether making a formal presentation or just having a conversation, make communication a performance. Vary the pace of speech, vary the tone of your voice, add humour where appropriate, add serious points to draw the listener's attention back and leave breaks in delivery for the listener to absorb what you have said. Critique your own 'performance'. Are you bored listening to you? If you are, you can guarantee most of your audience will be too. Common sense tells us that, if a message is naturally boring (pages of statistics, dates and times), it is better delivered in a different way (in this instance, perhaps a document followed by a discussion). Even an Oscar-winning actor would struggle to make a sheet of figures gripping. The ability to make communication an engaging performance comes from an inner confidence that it's ok to use your rich, emotional human being side to 'play' with your ideas in public. Why not?

Find personal links: People prick up their ears and focus most readily when listening to an issue in which they have a personal interest. It's surprising how a previously bored companion can become suddenly interested when the conversation switches to something close to his heart. If you want to turn on the 'ears' of another, think of a way your message can be linked to his interests. This will provide 'hooks' on which to hang your ideas. You may have to do some work first to find these hooks but there's no need to be sneaky about this. Simply ask your audience (whether that's one person or many) about their specific interests in a topic or what they would like to get out of a meeting, then tailor your input accordingly. If this were done more often, meetings would be shorter and more productive and there would be fewer yawns all round.

Prepare your body and your voice: The newest people on the communication training circuit are professional actors – and they have much to teach us. Only a foolhardy thespian would go on stage without preparing himself for a performance. The actor prepares his thinking for the role (who am I playing?). He then prepares his body and his voice (a tense throat cannot produce volume or colour). Finally, he will make sure he knows his words. You may be this disciplined when preparing for a formal presentation but how good are you at preparing for an important conversation? Good communicators take a few minutes to focus their thinking before a meeting. They shake off the mental clutter that would otherwise follow them – the earlier row with a colleague, the traffic jam on the way to the office, the work that needs to be completed by tomorrow morning. They recognise how this clutter, and the anxieties about the forthcoming meeting itself, can show up in their body and affect their ability to be heard. If you are keen on physical fitness, I'm sure you already know simple ways of gaining physical composure but for the uninitiated it's worth learning a few quick and simple relaxation procedures to enable you to get your body under physical control. Similarly, if you suffer with a shaky voice or tend to have a dull delivery, reading aloud, or singing, is a good way of strengthening your voice and learning to be more expressive. Reading children's stories is particularly good for this and has the added benefit of pleasing the little ones in your household.

Prepare your 'script': For formal presentations, you may feel the need for detailed notes or a script. There are definite pros and cons to this. On the plus side, the act of preparing notes will help you structure your thinking, clarify the content and remember it. On the downside, delivering directly from a script tends to make the delivery stilted, inviting the audience to make up on lost sleep. An actor reading his lines is not as natural and convincing as one who knows them by heart, leaving him free to focus on an engaging delivery. Of course, an actor is trained to do this and has developed an excellent memory in the process. For most non-thespians, it's more manageable to go half way – prepare in detail but learn by heart only the themes and structure you want to cover and then speak spontaneously from the heart. Use your brief notes as a prompt only when needed. If you stumble, go off at a tangent or decide on a new point you hadn't thought of before, your audience will be none the wiser to your changes. Make it clear that you believe in what you say and in your right to say it and your audience will sit up and hear your message.

The organisation communication paradox

Most organisations spend a considerable amount of time and money trying to improve communication. They invest in directors of communication, communication newsletters, noticeboards, cascade briefing sessions, communication conferences, upward forward downward and sideways feedback, presentation training courses, e-communication workshops and plenty more besides. Yet, despite these valiant attempts, poor communication still crops up as a problem area in staff surveys and team reviews. The familiar cry of *'we want more communication'* has made some CEOs despair, not knowing what to try next, while others choose to ignore these demands – *'well, they always say that so it doesn't mean anything'*. From a human being standpoint, everything means something but not always what it at first appears. So, what does the repeated demand for communication really mean?

In most instances, it doesn't mean staff want another corporate newsletter, employee handbook or film of the CEO's latest speech. All these things can be valuable in their own right but this isn't what the demand for communication is about. The underlying message is a cry not for information but for *inclusion*. This demand relates to the human desire to have control over one's life, to decide the direction of change; let us have our say and be heard so that we can be the co-creators of our destiny. As noted in the previous chapter, to be without control, like flotsam and jetsam on a beach, is psychologically destructive and diverts attention along either of two paths. It can lead to a pattern of giving up (why should I bother? what's the point?), where an air of resignation leads to a minimal level of performance and no more. Alternatively, it prompts a shift of focus towards activities aimed at regaining control. Energy is deflected from the goals of the organisation towards more political ambitions. Hence, the ongoing demand for more communication is about much more than a request for information. It's about people asking to be recognised as living and breathing, thinking and feeling human beings.

Truly effective leaders and managers understand this human being dimension. They have a sincere belief in respect and curiosity and communicate accordingly. They walk the talk at a personal level and they discipline those who do not behave likewise. They build a culture in which respect is a natural way of working. They communicate constantly by their sincere engagement with their people, at all levels. When people speak, they listen. When people don't speak, their views are requested. Communication is an everyday interaction. It's the culture of an organisation in words and deeds. It's what human beings do. One-off, 'staged' communication initiatives fool no one. That's why they don't work. Funny, then, that organisations spend so much money on them.

What next?

Creating the work environment in which people can deliver at their best must have, as its starting point, the answer to one fundamental question – what's all this communicating, rushing about, performing, developing and delivering for?

CHAPTER 13

Harnessing Motivation: The Importance of Purpose

P urpose matters to human beings. While short-term goals like getting the next promotion or buying a new house may fill our heads on a day-to-day basis, purpose concerns a more fundamental matter. It answers the question 'what's the point in me?' It's not so fundamental that it explains the meaning of life, the universe and everything. It's more the meaning of our life in our own personal universe. Purpose is big and deep but highly individual. It gives us a compass to guide us and pulls us back when we go off track. If we don't know the way, then purpose helps us find it. It's the basis for motivation, why we put our energy behind one thing and not another. If purpose is missing, as soon as we lift our heads out of the crazy busy-ness of short-term goals, there's a vacuum. Lack of an overarching purpose is the reason why we can feel down after the successful completion of a major project at work or at home. It's often the basis for many older people falling into depression if they have not re-established a new purpose having fulfilled their earlier roles.

Purpose isn't a single-headed beast. We can have a purpose for work, one for our home life, one for our spiritual life and one for our social life and they may all fit together like charming Russian dolls. Alternatively, they can be akin to the like-poles of magnets, pushing us in different directions, each purpose jostling with the others for priority. For example, if I work very long hours to fulfil my work purpose but rarely see my family, I can't fulfil the purpose I have in mind for parenthood. Something will have to be adjusted if I am to get the closest fit between both ideas of purpose. This is far from a simple task such that the act of creating, adjusting and readjusting the different strands that make up a sense of purpose can be the work of a lifetime.

In his book *The Purpose Economy*, Aaron Hurst[45] outlines five myths that help to clarify what purpose is and is not. In his view, it is not: a cause, a luxury for the wealthy, equivalent to a revelation, limited to certain jobs, or easy to find or follow. It is: a whole approach to work and to serving others (a verb, not a noun), a need that is universal to us all, a journey not a destination, a part of every role not just those that appear socially laudable, and worth the effort that is required. To Hurst, purpose is something to be found in all that we do. It encompasses what matters to us individually but, in addition, the process of moving towards that purpose may have a positive impact on what matters to others. Having purpose is usually win-win.

Purpose matters to organisations too. It provides the all-encompassing direction that makes sense of prevailing goals, activities, priorities, culture and so forth. It's the foundation on which strategy is built and co-ordinates the effort of an organisation's members towards the same aim. Just as for an individual, organisation purpose answers the 'why' question. Why are we doing this and why are we not doing that? And, just as for an individual, an organisation's purpose cannot be set in stone. It needs to be revisited, reshaped and kept alive.

Where is individual purpose found?

Human beings derive their purpose, or purposes, from their core needs set against the backdrop of their own moral code. You didn't know you were so clever, did you? From early on in childhood, our experiences shape our ambitions. *What do you want to be when you grow up?* is a common question to ask a young child and reflects the soup of implicit expectations fed to children and young people by parents, school and society about what should be achieved. Then, as we bump along in life, with our core needs constantly demanding attention, experience teaches us the difference between what's 'nice to have' and what's 'essential'. Unfortunately, sometimes we learn this lesson too late to hang on to the essentials – we may have frittered them away or missed the opportunity to acquire them. If we're lucky, we're prompted by family, friends or an event to reflect on what matters to us most. This increase in awareness helps clarify the importance of balancing needs against each other. 'Having it all' is something few achieve. Fortunately, it's possible to learn to live a contented, purposeful life with one or more need unmet provided others are satisfied (e.g. perhaps I will never get the recognition I deserve at work but through work I can ensure the well-being of my loving family). To quote Aaron Hurst:

> *purpose comes when we know we have done something that we believe matters – to others, to society and to ourselves. From the small and mundane daily choices we make to systemic and*

historic impact, we strive to contribute to the well-being of the world around us. Societal purpose isn't isolated to volunteering and philanthropy, or careers in education and social work. While these often spark feelings of purpose, we can also derive purpose through decisions about how we consume, from decreasing your carbon footprint, to buying local produce at the farmer's market. We can also discover meaning through our daily work, where we help the people on our teams and provide consumers with our products and services.

Hurst, The Purpose Economy *(2014), p28*

Purpose and work

Deep reflection on purpose is not something most of us do often. Certainly, as I get up from my warm, snuggly bed on a cold winter's morning, eat my breakfast and drink my coffee at breakneck speed, rush out to scrape the ice from the car then file into the station car park with a line of others juggling for parking spots before squeezing myself uncomfortably close between two other people I don't know on a crowded train on my way to work, I am unlikely to be thinking 'oh good, another day at the office to fulfil my purpose and meet my needs. Whoopee.' In truth, I'm unlikely to be thinking about much at all other than hoping the individual next to me with a serious halitosis problem gets off soon. On an average day, most of us just get on with our work lives without considering why we're doing what we're doing. It's only when things get tough or opportunities come along to change role or when someone directly asks us that awkward question 'what do you want from your job?' that we dip our toes into these murky waters. So here is that awkward question – why do we work?

The simplest explanation is that the incentive for work outweighs the downsides of early morning starts, horrendous commuting and a myriad of other negatives. If it wasn't in our interest to work, we wouldn't do it. At a basic level, working equates with survival. If this is the only job available and I need to feed my family, then this is the job I have to do. Sadly, there are still many adults, and in some circumstances children, who work in conditions that range from hazardous to inhumane just to fill their stomachs. Even when there is a benefit system to provide support and the fear of basic survival is lifted, holding on to a job, any job, can be critical. It's most concerning that an estimated 20% of the UK population have no savings to draw on if made redundant.[46]

Lottery winners aside, maintaining a regular income is important to most of the working age population. Yet, money acts as an incentive for more than just our financial security. It's also a measure of recognition and status and acts as a gateway into different lifestyles. But, as the saying goes, money isn't everything. A high level of pay alone is not enough to secure a well-motivated workforce (though undoubtedly it helps). Once security needs are met, human beings want more than positive bank balances. The other core needs are hungry and want recognition too.

The aim: congruence of purpose

We may not start each day with the conscious determination that our purpose will be achieved but we probably know when the road we're travelling on is headed in the wrong direction. The realisation that work isn't what we'd hoped for can come as a sudden awakening, like the flick of a light switch, or as a growing awareness akin to watching sunset fade into night. The degree to which our needs are satisfied depends on what's going on inside us and what's going on in our environment, leaving much scope for things to change. In some roles and on some days we hit the jackpot and all our core needs are met. On other days or in other jobs we have to compromise. In bleak moments, none of our needs are met; this is not a good place to be and usually leads to misery all round and to long stints at the bar.

When each need is met, our motivation will be at its highest because life feels good, or good enough, in most respects. Here is the seat of purpose – what it's all for, even if we don't label it as such. Reaching this nirvana is dependent on the interaction of the individual and the work environment. If my purpose is sufficiently aligned with my employer's purpose, I have a higher chance of achieving my goals and, in return, the organisation will have captured my energy and enthusiasm for its aims. When our purposes differ significantly, we will both struggle. As a manager, if you are to help your people give of their best, you will have to consider whether there is snug fit between individual and organisation purpose or if the differences between them are irreconcilable. It's unlikely that a job description, corporate handbook or organisation mission statement will help much in this task. An attractive document that states how an organisation *will* be, and how its people *should* behave within it, does not in itself mean I will believe what is says, agree with it or make it part of 'me'. The everyday behaviour of senior leaders and managers is far more potent in shaping a view of an organisation's real purpose than that espoused on paper. It's worth remembering here that for individuals 'the organisation' is not necessarily the whole enterprise but the part of it with which they interact – their team, their department and their network. As a manager, your behaviour indicates the organisation's purpose to those around you.

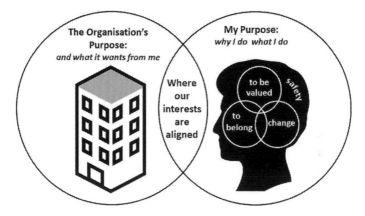

FIGURE 3: The alignment of purpose

Congruence of purpose comes from the ability to marry both head and heart in the aims of the organisation, as shown by a recent survey by the CIPD.[47]

> When we explored shared purpose in our case study organisations, it seemed strongest when employees developed an emotional connection with it. You could argue that this is easier for some of the public-sector organisations than some of our other case studies, but this is not necessarily the case. At Standard Chartered Bank, for instance, employees have an emotional connection with the bank's reputation and the many corporate social responsibility and volunteering opportunities that are open to them. At Pfizer, employees have an emotional connection with improving patients'

lives, and at Xerox Global Document Outsourcing Service Delivery team, employees have a strong bond around providing excellent customer service.

CIPD Shaping the Future Report

Sustainable Organisation Performance. What Really Makes the Difference (2011)

Of course, identifying a purpose doesn't automatically mean that it can be achieved. If I know what I need to feel satisfied but progress towards it is painfully slow, my motivation will eventually ebb away. When the question 'what's the point of me here?' doesn't have a sound answer, my focus will soon shift elsewhere. Swimming against the organisational tide is rarely a long-term option.

Helping individuals define their purpose

Individual purpose isn't something that can be established on the run. It needs time and a good degree of challenge and reflection. Ideas have to be tested out. Do they feel right? Is there more about this purpose business than I have been willing to consider, more beneath the surface than my first analysis suggests? Indeed, have I ever really thought about my purpose at all? Alas, in the work environment, the act of reflection is often relegated to a *nice-to-have-if-we-only-had-the-time* activity. We're all so busy *doing* that we don't have much time for *being*. Reflection is a *being* activity and it isn't complicated. It only requires a willingness to put matters on hold so that they can be looked at from a range of angles. The recent interest in mindfulness (mostly meditation under a new name) is beginning to show how the ability to pause our activity and our thinking has positive effects for health and for decision-making.[48] By taking time out from frenetic action, we have a better chance of allowing our head and heart to connect, to bring what we think we want close to what we feel is right.

To be meaningful, purpose must be personal, not a list of work objectives and targets. Defining individual purpose turns the tables and asks what a human being aims to achieve from work, not what the organisation wants from him. As a manager, you can help your team members consider their purpose by giving them the time, space and encouragement to do so but don't think that this can be accomplished by a one-off agenda item at a meeting. It will need to be a rolling task, visited and revisited on many occasions. It will need the word *purpose* to become part of the everyday office lexicon, not a concept taken out of a metaphorical box on awaydays. It will require a clear explanation of why you believe purpose to be important, consideration of confidentiality issues, then sensitive handling and more of the other P-word, patience.

Defining purpose is a challenge that will be met in a variety of ways by individual team members so expect the purpose of one person to look different from that of another, with varying degrees of completeness. To encourage people in this task, be open about your own broader life goals. Tell stories about your purpose because this implicitly gives your team members permission to talk about themselves in a more personal light. There is one essential here. Whatever the outcome of this process, you must respect it. You might give a nudge to someone if you think they've missed the point of the exercise but who are you to tell them that their personal purpose is wrong? You are also likely to have people who are not willing to share their purpose with you. So be it. That's their right. But even if you only get an inkling of what matters to the members of your team you will be in a better place to create an environment that will motivate them. You will also know if the path your organisation is following has the scope to fulfil the needs of your people provided, that is, if you know where that path is leading.

Organisation purpose

The one element of purpose that most organisations share is their desire to survive. There are few examples of organisations that deliberately want to put themselves out of business except in cases of fraud, where lining the senior executives' pockets is the key goal, or where success means eradicating a problem the organisation was set up to solve. For example, the vision of the Roll Back Malaria Partnership is, valiantly, 'of a world free from the burden of malaria'. When their mission is accomplished, and they are on the way towards this (hooray), their job will be done – no more organisation. However, there aren't many situations like this so we can assume that survival is on the agenda of most organisations. Even when a victim of its own success, an organisation will usually choose to morph into another entity rather than sign its own death warrant. Coram, a children's charity, originated as a Foundling Hospital 275 years ago but, as hospitals of this nature were phased out, it evolved to offer adoption and family support services instead and is still thriving today. The Dupont organisation was founded in 1802 and originally produced gunpowder but, when forced by the US government to divest itself of much of its production, it diversified into what has become a broad range of science and engineering businesses. Even though the lifespan of major organisations has shortened considerably over the past fifty years, like people, organisations want to live.

Beyond survival, the notion of organisation purpose appears less clear cut. A quick perusal of FTSE 100 company websites shows how confusing the notion of organisation purpose can be, with the terms *purpose*, *vision* and *mission* often used interchangeably. The mix-up of nomenclature doesn't matter in itself but it does reflect a certain shallowness of thinking when it comes to choosing what purpose is all about – and purpose is a matter of choice, not a given, as shown by how changing trends in business thinking affect an organisation's stated reason for doing what it's doing. At one point, purpose was about making or delivering the best of whatever it is that an organisation does. Then the mantra became the drive for growth, then the drive for efficiency, then the focus shifted to shareholder value, then to putting the customer first and so on. There is no right or wrong in this, except that the search for a single simple solution to purpose can quickly lead to a bias in perspective and a partial view.

To create a sustainable entity, purpose must balance the interests of all bodies who have a concern in that organisation continuing to function. Critical to this, however, is the requirement that, as circumstances alter, this balancing act allows for a redistribution of how these interests are met. At some point, even those who currently gain the most, and who are likely to hold power, may have to learn to share.

But wait a minute, I hear you cry. Surely the purpose of a commercial business is just to make money, albeit in a sustainable way. Unquestionably so, but the real question is to make money for whom? Employees get paid, suppliers earn a living, shareholders get their dividend, traders earn their keep by buying and selling shares, banks make money by lending it, customers get value for money, society gets fewer people in the benefits system – all have a stake in profit, though in different forms. And don't think the public sector is excluded from the notion of profit because, while it is not a purpose in itself here, good housekeeping is, so swop happy shareholders for happy taxpayers, or happy donors to charities. All stakeholders, as individuals and as collective bodies, should have an interest in an enterprise continuing in an economically sound manner. But purpose can, and in my view should, be about so much more than money. The interests of individuals, groups, societies and the wider world ought to be reflected in the reason for an organisation's existence. Then, for an organisation to be sustainable, it must reflect these interests in the way its purpose is lived out.

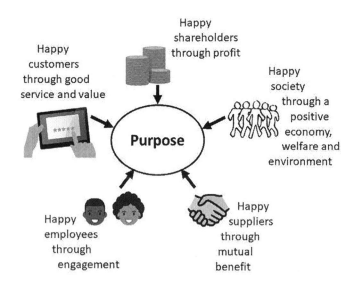

FIGURE 4: The many faces of purpose

To return to the FTSE 100 companies, the degree to which different stakeholders are included in their stated organisational purpose varies greatly. I suspect that, if quizzed, the CEOs of these businesses would say that one could 'take it as read' that the other groups are included – but are they? For instance, while clients are often referenced, employees often are not. How can this be? At whatever level they are employed, workers are interested in the overarching purpose of the organisation because it dictates whether they can achieve their own goals (if an organisation decides it no longer needs psychologists, I'm looking for another job).

Whichever way a purpose is presented, the words that are heralded in public (let's call this the public relations or PR purpose) may be a long way from the purpose employees see lived out each day (the cut-the-crap or CTC purpose) and the gap between the two can be sizeable. Consider the recent PPI and mortgage mis-selling scandals, which exposed the informal purpose of some organisations as deliberately exploiting customers. Similarly, the LIBOR (London interbank offered rate) fixing scandal that affected the broader business environment showed an accepted purpose of 'gain of a few' over the interests of the many. Common supermarket buying practices suggest a purpose close to blackmailing suppliers – pay us this extra lump sum or we won't stock your goods. The behaviour of senior business teams allocating themselves salaries and benefit packages beyond any logical justification suggests a purpose of dislocating reward from the real value of the people filling the role. These activities were not encoded in a formal purpose but were considered fair play in the organisations in which they occurred. So, when we read the fine PR words of purpose, human beings are right to question whether they have any relationship to the real world they experience. When there is a significant gap between what is said and what is done, senior teams seem to assume that their employees are highly gullible. That they believe the PR version. Well, be warned. Human beings nearly always see through pretence. They may choose to play along with it but don't mistake this with being blind to the reality.

And what if people no longer want to play along? Soon, senior managers may have no choice but to broaden their view of purpose if they are to attract and retain the bright stars needed to keep an organisation alive. From those fortunate enough to be economically secure, there is a growing clamour for more than salary and status. To feel satisfied and engaged, today's young people seek to find a purpose in their work beyond profit and some are beginning to forgo once-enticing high salaries, and accompanying frenetic lifestyles, to build a broader sense of personal value. Making an impact beyond their own bank balance is becoming a central theme to the career aspirations of many.

Creating a human being purpose

There is another angle that can be taken when creating purpose. If the organisation purpose seems too distant from the needs of your team members, or doesn't ring their emotional bell, you can create something that's easier to relate to and that has a more motivating edge. A 'human being purpose' is a separate ambition, agreed by all team members, which runs in parallel with the organisation purpose, along the lines of 'we'll do this for the business and we'll also do this for ourselves'. But, and it's an important but, different purposes (individual, organisation and human being) must not compete. Teams that work primarily for their own interests tend to create their own demise. The aim is to find points at which different interests coincide or at least work in harmony. Examples of a human being purpose might be 'no team member will be unduly stressed by an unmanageable workload' or 'all team members will experience meaningful development to support their key career goal during the next year' or simply 'we'll have fun in all we do and if work loses its sense of fun, we'll stop and ask why'. So far, so bland. Along with your team members, you will then need to turn these general goals into specific actions. What development? How will stress levels be monitored? What will the practical response be to a high-stress alert? How will we know if we're having fun? And so on. As a manager, you'll need to inspire your people to find this version of purpose. This kind of thinking doesn't emerge from a dull, computer-led approach. It needs heart, sincerity, commitment, and most of all it needs you to demonstrate that you're serious about it. If you treat it as airy-fairy, fluffy stuff, your staff will too and if you create it then file it away, don't expect much engagement in your next initiative. But, if you ground this human being approach with real examples and practical actions that make a difference to how people feel about their roles, you will see the difference in their motivation and performance.

The key to a human being purpose is that it recognises that people are people, not human resources, human capital, or part of the organisation's greatest asset. They are people with hearts and minds and human needs. Meet those needs and people will reward an organisation with their energy and loyalty.

The cost of losing focus on purpose

Lack of clarity around organisation purpose leads to confusion, duplication, waste and more. It provides fertile ground for short-term thinking, strategy that shifts with the sands (well, with every change of CEO) and costly initiative overload. You will have noticed that, despite this, in the commercial world performance can roll along quite nicely for years with a muddy or absent purpose. At some point, however, problems do arise, whether in the form of a gradual decline or an emergency. If it's not too late, drastic action may get the organisation back on track, rather like a last-minute tug on a steering wheel when a driver is about to nod off. However, if the driver doesn't wake up, there'll be a crash. No wonder organisational lifespan is decreasing. Lack of clarity about fundamental purpose costs organisations money. For employees, it costs jobs.

A recent survey of 474 executives from around the world by the EY Beacon Institute and Harvard Business Review Analytic Services[49] found that 90% of respondents said their company recognised the importance of purpose for the success of their business. However, just 46% reported that purpose informed their strategic and operational decision-making. As the report notes, this is an opportunity missed. More compelling is the finding that the companies where a strong sense of purpose had been established had significant advantages in terms of their ability to undertake transformational change, drive successful innovation and deliver consistent revenue growth. The survey clearly demonstrates that purpose is not just something to have in order to tick the good leadership box. It impacts directly on the bottom line and hence the long-term sustainability of an entity.

Remember, that the call for purpose is not about finding one idea and sticking to it regardless. It is a demand for focus, a well-considered perspective on what matters most for all stakeholders, and a willingness to flex how an organisation operates to keep this focus as the driving force behind everything it does.

And what about the cost to customers? In the public sector, where demands are high and rising, money is inadequate and the work is often complex, a confused purpose can have a significant impact on the welfare of the human beings receiving a service or even put lives at risk. A few years ago, I had the opportunity to read the draft strategy document for adult care services in a local authority. While the plans given were mostly laudable, the objective of each initiative was written in terms of policies to be introduced. Nowhere in the document was the overriding purpose of the service given – to enable a higher quality of life, health and well-being for those in need of support. When I mentioned this to the chief executive, his words were along the lines of 'oh that's a good idea. I must make a note of that.' How extraordinary that the notion of including the real purpose of the service was a novel idea. The existing purpose was focused on the creation and adherence to policies and procedures in line with government guidelines. The real purpose of these policies and procedures had got lost along the way, and not because the people were bad-hearted or didn't care but because they had been sidetracked. When the pressure is on, adherence to policies and procedures and the achievement of short-term goals often overshadow a greater sense of purpose, becoming purposes in themselves. When *that's the way we always do it* is more important than *why are we doing it at all?* an organisation has a problem.

The consequence of losing sight of purpose is to forget that human beings are at the end of the purpose chain. When this happens, people are regarded as objects without hearts, emotions or personal lives. They are statistics, suppliers, clients, customers, patients or employees but they are not human beings, people like us. The performance of individuals and the organisation overall should be assessed against its purpose, not against processes or policies or procedures. Government bodies, leaders of many public-service organisations and business leaders would benefit from going back to the fundamental question of their purpose if they are to meet the real needs of their many stakeholders.

What's this got to do with me – I'm only a manager?

You may feel that the issue of organisation purpose is above your pay grade. Leaders are responsible for setting purpose and strategy, are they not? Certainly but maybe, after a promotion or two, you will fill that role. Then you will have the responsibility for setting direction and encouraging an organisation of human beings to follow you. But don't wait until then. If you're a manager, you're managing someone or something. Recognise your span of influence and aim to instil a sense of purpose here. You can determine a purpose for yourself and a human being-focused purpose for your area of responsibility. You can encourage individual team members to reflect on their ambitions and visions for the future. To your people, your actions represent the organisation's purpose. If the direction of your actions spins with the wind, you will have a confused team. If they fit within a coherent and well-communicated purpose, you allow your team members to channel their effort in one direction.

How to foster a sense of purpose

There's little point helping people to establish a personal purpose at work if the wider organisation/department/function/ team purpose within which it sits is not defined because each perspective is required to make sense of the work puzzle. To help your team clarify their purpose, challenge yourself to do the following:

Revisit the purpose of the organisation you work for: Has the organisation purpose been clearly articulated? Have you assumed what it is without checking? If there is a defined purpose, how close are the PR and the CTC versions? Consider how to translate this general purpose so that it has specific meaning for your team. Does your role support the overarching purpose – if not, why are doing what you're doing?

Find the courage to challenge those above you for answers: If there had been more challenge about purpose in the financial services industries, fewer large fines might have been incurred. If there had been more challenge about purpose in care homes, hospitals and local authorities, or to those supposed to oversee quality, our elderly folk, our disabled children, our sick family members and those in need might have received better care. If there had been more challenge about purpose in the banking sector, I wouldn't have received over fifty calls asking me to make a PPI claim.

Think beyond your immediate boundaries: Consider the wider system in which you operate. What is the true purpose of the stakeholders with whom you interact, whether these are other departments, suppliers, contractors or customers? How does their purpose impact on the purpose of your team/your organisation?

Think beyond your immediate organisation: What is happening in business, social and political environments that could affect your purpose? Your team and your organisation do not float freely in space. They exist in a world where little is static. Think ahead to potential scenarios for the future. You cannot predict what is to come but you can prepare your team for a variety of possibilities. Scenario planning is wonderful discipline. Read up about it.

Involve your staff in crafting an overall purpose for the team: You can't impose purpose so you may as well get your team in on the act. Be creative in how you approach the task and be as whacky as your team will allow to draw in both heart and computer. Visual cues are often better at stimulating the imagination than words alone. And don't be too worried about wordsmithing a perfect document. Purpose doesn't have to be written as a clever one-liner. It doesn't have to fit any fixed format. This is not for marketing. It's for you and your team.

Create a human being purpose: Take the extra time to add the human element to your team purpose. It might be just a paragraph or a stand-alone document but, whatever it turns out to be, make sure it's something that is practical and you have the will and commitment to follow through.

Encourage individual members of your team to consider the main strands of their own purpose at work: How do your people see themselves developing in the short and long term? What picture do they hold of the person they want to be in the future? What do they want from their role and from the organisation, or elsewhere, to make this possible?

Check for a good fit: When you've got that far, give some one-to-one time to individual team members to help them consider how their own ambitions fit, or don't, within your team and the wider organisation. Is there scope for people to meet their needs within the overall remit of your team? What has to be put in place to make this possible? What are the potential consequences of a bad fit? If a team member wants more than is possible, then it's better for all concerned that this is made clear.

Use purpose: The reason for identifying the purpose of an organisation is not to provide window dressing for the annual report or a website. It's because the real purpose provides a reference point against which actions can be compared. Every activity should be considered against this purpose and questions asked if it is found wanting. To be worthy of the time invested in defining it, purpose has to be a living ideal. Refer to it when planning ahead. Challenge people against it. Debate it regularly. Relate staff performance to it. Make it live.

What next?

You know where you want to get to and it's going to take effort, skill and commitment to get there. You're up for the journey but how do you get your team to go with you?

CHAPTER 14

Helping Human Beings to Give of Their Best

Think of the times when you've been on top form, when achieving your mental to-do list was within your grasp, when the goals you achieved were satisfying and worthwhile, when progress was visible, when the people you worked with seemed to be as much companions as colleagues and when feedback from your manager was dotted with praise. These may be the moments we dream about yet work doesn't have to be perfect to create the feeling 'this is how things are meant to be'. The balance of ups and downs needs only be just in favour of the ups to make us approach our place of work with a slight spring in our step. As a manager, you play a critical role in creating the environment necessary to foster this sense of satisfaction and, if you achieve this, you will also have generated a strong momentum for performance.

What do we mean by 'managing performance'?

The term 'managing performance' raises some interesting questions. What happens when performance is not managed?

Do we run amok? Does performance disappear? Are we left as waxworks, fixed in a distorted and rather shiny reality of ourselves? If we manage 'performance' as part of an employee's behaviour, what are we not managing?

Of course, there are behaviours that we bring to the office and behaviours that we leave at home. As a manager, you will be thankful you don't have to take responsibility for the domestic lives of your staff. My manager may say to me 'how are you?' but I suspect he'd rather not get chapter and verse on the vagaries of my children, the state of my overgrown garden or my undergrown bank balance. As an employee, I know the rules. I bring to work what is relevant and leave the rest at home. You may be a confirmed slipper-wearer in the comfort of your own sitting room but I suspect you do not bring your red silk slippers with the purple pom-poms to the office, even if you'd like to. Yet, home life undoubtedly influences work and work life influences home and there's the rub. We often bring more to work than we realise. We may leave the actual slippers behind but we may bring an emotional longing for their comfort and ease with us. As a manager, although you are not responsible for solving my specific home life problems, when you talk about managing my performance you're managing most of me in the process, at least for the hours that I'm employed. I am not two people; I am one. Managing performance equates with managing whole human beings.

The 'computer' approach to managing performance

While the language of performance management has changed over the years, and its reach has extended to cover both the *what* and the *how* of work, the drive to analyse, standardise and measure remains. Performance management still comes from a heavily computer-led stance.

This factual, rational approach is favoured for a good reason. Standardised frameworks create a common language, enabling the coordination of initiatives for appraisal, development, reward, recruitment, promotion, 360° feedback, assessment centres, talent management and succession planning and anything else that moves or breathes. They allow all these activities to be tied together with coordinated threads. What's more, on paper or more often in clever software packages, these threads can be neatly aligned and ordered. In theory, the result of all this sophisticated work should be the best possible performance management system. Unfortunately, owing to two significant problems, such perfection is not so easily attained. Firstly, common frameworks are based on the idea that the roles, and the environment in which these roles take place, are more or less static and, as noted too many times already, our world does not stand still. The *what* and the *how* required in our work can, and do, change regularly in response to pressure from a wide range of external and internal factors. Indeed, it's not unusual for the ink to be barely dry on a new performance management system before its users clamour for amendments. Secondly, and of far greater importance, is that most approaches to performance management pay little heed to *why* – why individuals should want to do what is asked of them?

Perhaps that's the reason that so many people, staff and their managers alike, dread the appraisal season – that time of year when managers and individuals take stock of their performance. You may feel this is simply because it adds an extra load to their already busy work life. Or maybe it's because the process feels disconnected from the reality of what goes on each day. Or maybe it's because nothing much happens afterwards; the hoped-for two-way feedback, development plans, salary increase, promotion or whatever may not materialise. Whatever the reason, performance management processes, such as appraisal, risk becoming an end point in their own right, coming adrift from their intended purpose, as illustrated in recent research by Deloitte Consulting LLP and Bersin by Deloitte[50] designed to identify the top twelve global business challenges in talent management, leadership and HR. By surveying over 2,500 business and HR leaders in ninety-four countries, they found that only 8% of respondents viewed their performance management process as an effective way of driving high levels of business value. Indeed, nearly 60% rated existing approaches as weak at driving engagement and high performance and the same percentage rated it as weak in terms of an effective use of time. Awareness that current processes are not up to the job intended may account for why over 70% of respondents were in the process of, or had already completed, a review of their performance management systems. Some have already jettisoned their old ways and replaced them with more flexible, ongoing, skills-based conversations with a strong coaching ethos. The Deloitte survey recognises the need for senior executives to roll up their sleeves and do some deep thinking about what performance management is all about.

A 'heart and computer' approach to performance management

At its root, to be effective, performance management needs to be more than objective setting and appraisal. It needs to be personal. To harness energy, motivation, will and belief in a shared ambition, emotion as well as logic is needed. The computer approach suggests that people will do what is asked of them because it makes logical sense to act in the organisation's best interest. In short, they will comply. The heart approach suggests that if their personal interests, in addition to pay and rations, are met too, they will go beyond compliance; they will deliver with conviction. Attending to both heart and computer increases the chances of finding that elusive motivational high where both the organisation and the individual are satisfied. To reach this point, performance management must become less of a separate activity and more of a non-stop relationship between the individual and his manager. Managing performance from both our heart and computer requires ongoing dialogue. It asks for a willingness to get to know each other well enough so that what's hidden becomes clear. It's about both the manager and the individual changing to find the conditions needed for optimum performance. Reducing this to an infrequent, checklist-led discussion and an ongoing set of commands is too compartmentalised and oversimplified to enable people to work at their best.

Here's a thought. What if you consigned all the appraisal paperwork to the dustbin; how would your team members know what is required of them? What would you need to discover to find the elusive point at which different purposes overlap?

What implications would this have for your role? In case you were tempted, don't put the paperwork through the shredder just yet because that will only land you in hot water, but instead try to think as if the paperwork didn't exist. If there was no system to guide you, you would have to work from first principles and consider questions like these:

- Where are we going in the immediate and long term? Who is plotting our course?

- Are these destinations interesting enough to engage people?

- What talent do we have to make this journey possible?

- What conditions are needed to enable the talent to be used to the full?

Where are we going?

Put the future before the past: Many performance management systems lean heavily to the past rather than pull to the future. This isn't surprising as mixing the reward and planning aspects of performance in one process is likely to create bias. If I know my salary increase, promotion or job security depends on how you rate my past, then my attention will definitely be on that and not on future goals. In addition, thinking ahead is often more challenging than reviewing the past; it's easier to whizz by this section, set non-specified goals or to assume more of the same than do the hard thinking needed about the future. To avoid these problems, the two aspects of performance are better split. Reflection on the past should come after planning for the future. Why? Because, reward aside, the reason we review the past is to help people consider how to apply their skills to achieve future goals – those of the business and their own. This can't be done until the future direction has been agreed. What's more, any future direction consists of two elements – where we're going as a team/department and where I'm going as part of that enterprise.

Start from purpose: As discussed in the previous chapter, don't pass on a PR purpose if the human beings around you can sniff out a different, underlying agenda. This just insults their intelligence. From your experience, explain what the organisation really wants, the CTC purpose, even if it's not a good story to tell. You may have little choice over the general purpose and immediate goals of your organisation. However, you have considerably more choice over the human being purpose designed with your team. This purpose can motivate people even when the organisation's version is unpalatable or too distant to make any personal connection with your people. Human beings buy into this kind of purpose because it aims to allow everyone to make some progress towards their individual purpose.

Keep reviewing your plans: Whatever you do, don't be tempted to walk away once performance plans are formalised, even if you trust your team to deliver great things. Managers who are frantically busy and head down with their own set of tasks easily lose touch with what's happening on their patch. As a consequence, they are only alerted when there's an emergency and it's too late. What's more, at the moment you discover that an important project is falling apart you're unlikely to be in the best state to respond effectively because the anger, panic and fear triggered by unexpected events make for a poor management style. Try not to get caught up with so much activity that you give up on review and reflection. Someone needs to be looking where the team is headed. If you build in regular feedback loops, you will be kept abreast of progress and know when plans need to be adjusted. I'm aware that you have probably been told this many times before but ask yourself if you actually do it. Good managers keep a dialogue running between everyone involved; they allow others to contribute to decisions on the direction taken; they spot obstacles in the distance and change tack ahead of a potential collision. Make sure you lift your head out of the electronic in-tray of gloom to look ahead.

Are my people engaged?

Get to know how your people feel: Engagement is a feeling backed up by thoughts. If I give a rational explanation for why I am engaged but I don't have an emotional connection with this, I'm not engaged. Hence, you can only know if your people are truly with you if you know how they feel. Are your team members happy? Are they angry, disappointed, elated, numb or bored with the latest decisions from on high? How do they feel about their jobs and the path the team and the organisation are taking? To get to know the human beings who work in your team use the word *feel* rather than *think* (e.g. how do you feel about the new strategy?). I know it's become a bit of a joke to ask how people feel but jokes are often used to avoid difficult situations. If you can't use the word 'feel' without making a wisecrack, then it's quite likely you're not comfortable around emotion. That's something to work on if you want to grasp this human being stuff. If you do ask a question about emotion but you get a thinking reply ('I think it focuses on the right part of the market'), ask again ('but how do you feel about it?') until you get a feeling response (I feel disappointed that it's more of the same or I feel excited by what we're trying to achieve). To get to know the human beings you work with, you don't need to become their psychoanalyst; you just need to show genuine human interest. After all, we have already agreed that you're a human being yourself.

Get to know what your people value: Find out what matters most to your people in their work life beyond the specific tasks they have to complete. What matters least? What are the small things that make their life more difficult or make them feel appreciated or as if they matter little? What makes them feel unheard? If you don't ask, you will be a long time guessing.

Assume people work *with* you not *to* you: Not all types of engagement are the same. In a typical hierarchical organisation, it's easy for a parent–child style of engagement to take root. Being treated like a child is unlikely to keep high performers engaged for long. It also risks provoking a variety of unproductive, childish behaviour. Eric Berne,[51] the father of transactional analysis, brought to our attention how old patterns of learned behaviour can resurface in an instant when provoked by familiar triggers. If someone addresses me in a dominant, 'I know best and you don't' teacher-like way, they will sure-as-eggs get a stubborn, resistant and often badly behaved response from me. I am the youngest of three siblings and, as a child, I hated being put down. I'm not proud of my reaction but at least now I can recognise what's going on and deal with it. If, as a manager you behave as a parent, you are likely to trigger a range of childlike reactions and some of them will be decidedly unhelpful. Berne taught us that to allow human beings to act freely in the moment rather than be held in the traces of the past our interactions need to be adult-to-adult. To avoid the tendency to adopt a parental style, remind yourself that you work alongside your team not over it. Some team members may push and shove you into the parent role because it feels safest for them (as parents take responsibility) but resist this as it disempowers people and leaves you carrying the burden. To work in collaboration with your team rather than by command:

- agree the rules of your engagement with them, clarifying the type of support they need from you in order to deliver their goals and vice versa;

- identify when you need to sit on your hands and let your team get on without your interference; specify the boundaries of acceptable risk to allow this to happen;

- give your team permission to tell you when you are acting inappropriately as a parent (and don't send them to bed with no supper when they do).

What talent is at my disposal?

Growing talent isn't a science. It's an imprecise art involving an open mind, creative vision, juggling, quick reflexes, guesswork, eating humble pie when you get it wrong and, above all, a willingness to dedicate the time needed. When you get it right, it's immensely rewarding.

Understanding the skills and styles that people bring to work, the *how*, has enabled us to appreciate the types of talent needed for particular roles. The underlying methodology used to achieve this is often the competency or capability framework discussed in Chapter 5 along with role specifications that list the expert knowledge, skills and experience required. However, by defining the components of the *how* so precisely, if we're not careful we risk missing the point. When we examine human beings as a series of parts, it's easy to be deflected from seeing the interaction of these parts. It's a little like examining all the individual pieces of a jigsaw puzzle and ticking each off as present and correct without ever putting them together to see the picture they make. Human beings are not a series of parts that can be examined separately. We are made up of the interaction of our 'layers' – core needs, values and beliefs, styles and preferences and then behaviours – within the environment in which we operate. To help your people be at their best, you have to consider the complex web of this interaction. So, when it comes to developing talent, keep the following in mind.

Counter the itch for 10/10: Build teams with complementary skills. Identify the strengths and interests of your people because that's where their energy will lie. Stop looking for individuals to deliver in areas where they are weak. Do they really need to tick all the boxes or is a triple tick in a few areas enough? As long as you have the range of skills needed across team members, their coordinated effort should be able to deliver what is required.

Look for an individual's star talent: If an alien with no knowledge of management speak watched one of your team for a year from space, what would stand out as the individual's star feature, the edge from which they lead? How is this talent used to compensate for less strong areas? How can this talent be used to maximum effect? People often have skills and knowledge that are hidden, ignored or simply overshadowed. The most junior member of your team may be the best at chairing a meeting but never get a chance to do it. The receptionist may be a star amateur actor and a terrific public speaker but is kept at the front desk. What a waste.

Adjust the level of challenge: If you have people who do score 10/10, are they being stretched enough? How can you test them further to find their greatest skills? Can they take on more? The idea is not to smother them with more of the same (if you do, you'll soon find their resignation slip in your in-tray) but to add more complexity. If you aren't stretching and developing such people fast enough, why is that? Could it be that you feel threatened by their advancement? Do you need to let them go elsewhere if they are to use their potential to the full?

Look at the team profile: Given the purpose of your team, you need to know if the overall profile of talent at your disposal contains the capability needed to get the job done. Where you have skill gaps, plans will need to be in place to acquire or grow this capability or, at a minimum, flag up the risk this gap creates. A football team made up of brilliant defence players but without skill in other areas is unlikely to win many games.

Consider the broader life context: Consider performance against the backdrop of both an individual's immediate and longer-term goals, recognising that these might be vague. We don't all have neatly defined career plans. Ambitions that fire up our enthusiasm can take some time to establish but, if you never raise the subject and help people think this through, you may never see that fire at all. Be careful, though, not to impose your own desires on others. What creates sparks for one person may be the equivalent of a bucket of icy water for another.

If there are shortfalls in performance, be truthful: People usually know when their performance is lacking. A consistent behaviour problem indicates that an individual is stuck. If they could improve, they most probably would. As noted previously, when we're stuck we need to understand the type of glue keeping us rooted to the spot (or going around in circles). This takes more than simply describing what the problem looks like. Firstly, it needs honest information about the implications of the performance for the individual. Fudging feedback may make life easier on the day but will come back to bite you as that all-important companion, trust, will be the first casualty when the truth finally surfaces, leaving you with an additional problem to deal with. Secondly, it requires an investment of your time to investigate the root of the problem. The issue may be a straightforward lack of knowledge or skill or it may lie in the fuzzier areas of preference, emotion or motivation. If, through enquiry and listening, you can encourage some 'ah ha' new thinking, progress will be made. The glue will begin to unstick.

Clarify what you want: It's easy to spot when things are going wrong because, eventually, a problem gives you a kick in the shins and says 'I'm here!'. There's a consequence to failing performance whether it's a missed deadline, a sale lost, a project that didn't deliver, a customer complaint or something else. The benefit of hindsight then allows us to look back and say what ought to have happened. The wrong result helps us clarify the right one. What about when there isn't a problem? When you are starting from scratch to define what is needed in the future? That's a much tougher challenge and it's why future performance is often couched in general outcomes (e.g. improve your interactions with clients). Then, because expectations are not explicit, they tend to slip about like a moving target, making it difficult for an employee to hit the right spot with his performance. One of the most helpful interventions I've experienced as a coach is to prompt an individual and his manager to clarify exactly what this future performance should look like in practical terms, covering both the *what* and the *how*, so that they both agree what they're aiming towards (which clients? what kind of interactions? when? with what kind of feedback from the client? and so forth). It's extraordinarily easy to assume that we and our team members are thinking the same thing but performance cannot be managed on mere assumptions. Imagine if I needed a hip replacement on my left side but the surgeon assumed it was my right hip. His surgery might be of the highest standard but the outcome would be a disaster. Sounds unlikely? It's happened. To avoid your own version of mislocated surgery, ensure that you and your team members can fill in the blanks: *if this person performs as required, he will be doing this... and this... and this... with the result that...*

Have I created a performance-enhancing environment?

I hope that the brief sortie into core needs in earlier chapters will have given you ideas about how to foster an environment in which people can feel free to focus their attention and energy on work. By managing people in a way that creates a sense of safety, belonging, value and change, you stand the greatest chance of maximising their performance. You might also have a happier team and a happier self. Two reminders:

Agree your ground rules: Respect and curiosity are not prerequisites for managers only. They are required by all members of an enterprise. This human being business is not just down to you. Everyone in your team needs to buy into a human being-friendly way of working if it is to succeed. Make this a reality by crafting your ground rules together. Again, be as specific as possible.

Create joy: Ok, joy maybe going too far but ask yourself why work should be miserable or, if not that bad, just dull. This is life we're talking about. We're only here once, so isn't it a tragedy to spend that one life without fun or joy. Fear not, you don't need to hire a clown suit or have regular booze-ups to make this happen. Although a 'jolly' can help us all along from time to time, enjoyment doesn't come from one-off events. To foster enjoyment in the workplace, you will need to recognise that not everyone will find it in the same way. The type of joy that makes a long-term difference is rooted in everyday interactions. The more you smile and the more you focus on the positive, the more you enable your team to do the same. The more you recognise the upside, the more your team will have energy to tackle the downside. Enjoyment gives energy so how about spending a day when you informally monitor the amount of smiling and laughing in your team. How do you rate?

Your own mood will have significant impact on the mood of your people because bringing enjoyment to others is extremely difficult if you've lost your own sense of joy. If you feel miserable, you'll look miserable and convey a 'what's wrong?' rather than 'what's right?' attitude. Naturally, simply ordering yourself to cheer up is not the solution to feeling down. You have to work out what's going on in your 'heart' to create this feeling. The process to achieve this may be uncomfortable but ignoring the issue is unlikely to make it go away and, when you feel depressed or anxious, the already-heavy load of management seems heavier still. Invest time considering what makes you happy. If you need help to do this, that's a good thing. A trusted other can often help you to get to a better place more quickly than struggling on your own. As a well-known advertisement says, you're worth it.

Looking backwards: a word about reviewing past performance

Let's assume you have established a clear purpose for your team, that this has been translated into meaningful goals for all and that you have established the talent needed to deliver these goals. Now you come to the hard bit. You need to consider individual team members against this – who is skilled and motivated to take part in this plan and who is not fully there yet? This is where performance review comes in. Looking at the past shows us shortfalls in knowledge, skills and motivation that need to be addressed if future goals are to be met. That's the real point of looking back. Unfortunately, performance-related pay muddies the water here. To discuss the pros and cons of performance-related pay would fill a book in its own right but, by way of summary, as a method it cannot be relied upon to motivate.

Reward is a relative thing. Most of us consider the value of our pay and other benefits (known as our extrinsic reward as it comes from outside the person) motivating up to the point at which it equals our internal sense of what we, and the job we do, are worth. Whether adding more reward after this makes us more motivated is a moot point. Meta-studies looking at previous research on the subject suggest a weak link at best. Indeed, in some instances, adding more reward was found to decrease motivation. It seems that it's not possible to buy motivation with cash alone. To boost engagement with an enterprise such that people feel fully committed to its cause, managers must find ways of increasing the good feeling that comes from work itself (the intrinsic reward created by doing something we enjoy or feel to be worthwhile). We are back on the territory of core needs here. When work meets our core needs, we are more likely to feel satisfied, motivated and engaged and it's this engagement that leads to heightened performance.[52]

Be wary, then, of placing the emphasis in performance review heavily on financial reward for the past period because the positive glow that comes from a pay rise is temporary. If performance review only considers what the organisation wants, and not what the individual needs, your team members are unlikely to have the energy, let alone enthusiasm, to give of their best.

Making feedback work

Feedback is another word for conversation. When I talk with my family at the dinner table about my day, I'm giving them feedback about what happened to me. The stories I relate might involve them directly, perhaps concerning the dirty clothes they left on the bathroom floor that gave me extra work. Some stories might have no immediate link to them but have affected whether I'm grumpy, happy or exhausted that evening and explain why dinner is a frozen ready-meal or a freshly cooked favourite. My feedback on the day may also influence what will happen on the day to come. No more clothes on the bathroom floor, or else; the work assignment that kept me busy today will keep me busy for the rest of the week, and so on. In our household, we don't really call this giving feedback but that's exactly what we're doing. Everyone has a turn though, depending on their day, some may shout louder than others. What makes this a conversation is that it isn't one-way. My family make comments on my story, or my interpretation of it. Mealtimes are an interactive process of exchange with food thrown in. Research has shown that family meals, or the conditions that allow family meals to take place (i.e. it's not the food that makes the difference), are linked to healthier outcomes for children.[53] This isn't surprising. Spending time together and showing interest in each other's lives build security, belonging and personal value and help to support people through change and difficulty.

Work teams aren't that different from families. If the relationships in your team are to foster performance rather than hinder it, opportunities for meaningful and supportive conversations must exist. Giving feedback is part of this process but to work in your favour it needs to be ongoing, two-way and arise from a willingness to help. Blame rarely gets results.

Plan for feedback: When you need to give longish sessions of feedback, a good place to start is by completing this statement: *At the end of this feedback, I hope this human being leaves feeling... and knowing... because...* It's not a bad idea to complete it for yourself too – how do you want to feel and what do you want to know? If you can't complete this, wait until you can.

Work out how you feel about giving feedback: To make feedback work, you have to be in control of your emotions. If you are anxious, angry, irritated or in a hurry or simply don't give a damn, it's best to leave feedback for another day. You won't be able to listen and, as a human being, you will be at the will of your core needs which will knock your 'computer' off balance. This is where it all goes wrong! You need to be in good shape to draw on the essential feedback prerequisites of respect and curiosity. Respect allows us to give information without diminishing the value of the human being before us. Curiosity makes us seek to understand the human being better and to find creative ways forward. Take your time to get your heart and computer in a good place before embarking on feedback.

Be selective: Because you can give feedback on every aspect of an individual's performance doesn't mean you should. Stress the information that will make most difference. The rest can be left. Information overload will only lessen the individual's ability to absorb the most valuable feedback – it just creates extra material for the heart to filter and risks losing the key message in the process.

Make reviewing performance a constant two-way process: Remember, reviewing performance is something to do *with*, not *to*, an individual. It's your chance to learn about your management style as much as it's about the performance of the individual because the two are inextricably linked. If you work on an annual appraisal schedule, and that's the only time your team members get feedback, don't expect optimum performance. You'll be lucky just to get by. Some major organisations are now taking note of this. For example, in 2016 the consultancy firm Accenture announced it would disband its 'once-a-year evaluation process and implement a more fluid system, in which employees receive timely feedback from their managers on an ongoing basis following assignments' (Accenture CEO Pierre Nanterme, *The Washington Post*, 21 July 2015).

Don't be a slave to the paperwork: Any conversation about performance should be driven by its true purpose, not simply by the need to fill in a form. You might have to put in a little creative overtime to complete the forms at a later stage but don't let the paperwork 'tail' wag the review 'dog'.

Don't assume intention: Although it's tempting, don't give feedback on intent (you did that because...). Your guess might well be right but it's a high-risk strategy to suggest you know what's going on in another person's head. You are not party to all the factors that influence their life. If you want to know why someone did something, you only have to ask.

Add colour and detail rather than ratings: Give feedback in terms of real-life observable behaviour. When using 360° feedback, I have frequently heard individuals note that specific examples are more helpful than numerous ratings. Beautiful reports with lines of figures, bar charts and comparisons this way and that are whizzed by to get to the 'real' stuff at the back – what people said about behaviour. Why? Because ratings say little. Real-life descriptions convey much. Ratings also run the risk of looking accurate while hiding a wide range of bias. One study found idiosyncratic characteristics of the rater made up more than half of the variance of ratings given for performance, i.e. differences between raters accounted for more than the difference in the actual performance of the individuals.[54] Concerns with the potential inaccuracy, complexity and inefficiency of their rating-based performance management systems have led several organisations to jettison ratings in favour of more individualised approaches. Motorola, Microsoft, Adobe, Expedia and most recently Deloitte have joined this happy band.

> *Over the past few years the debate about performance management has been characterized as a debate about ratings – whether or not they are fair, and whether or not they achieve their stated objectives. But perhaps the issue is different:*

not so much that ratings fail to convey what the organization knows about each person but that as presented, that knowledge is sadly one-dimensional. In the end, it's not the particular number we assign to a person that's the problem; rather, it's the fact that there is a single number. Ratings are a distillation of the truth – and up until now, one might argue, a necessary one. Yet we want our organizations to know us, and we want to know ourselves at work, and that can't be compressed into a single number.

Buckingham & Goodall, Reinventing Performance Management. Harvard Business Review *(April 2015)*[55]

Invest enough time: The heart takes time to deal with feedback, both good and less good, so you need to build a timescale to allow for this. Skimping on time may prove costly in the long run.

It all starts with you

Helping people perform at their best at work is about helping them to be the best human being they can be. And that includes you. It's a tough message but there's no point in avoiding it. To find the sweet spot of performance where the needs of the individuals in your team and the needs of the organisation are balanced, you have first to understand your own needs. As their manager, you have a significant influence on the system in which your people operate. You may feel like a small cog in the larger machine of the organisation but, to your people, you hold an important key to the quality of their life at work. Unless you strive to get to grips with your own heart and computer, you will be intervening in their world as if wearing a blindfold. So, start with yourself. Test out your human being detective skills on you before applying them to your team. If you find this tricky, engage a friend to help you. Ask for feedback to inform you. Take time out to ponder. Grab a blank sheet of paper and draw four circles, each one representing a different human being layer. Then, add words or pictures to describe the different layers of you. No one is going to write on this with red pen, give you marks out of ten or ask you to do it again for homework. You are at liberty to make mistakes. In fact, I'd be surprised if you didn't change your picture many times before you end up with something that captures a smidgeon of the intricate, complex and unique human being that goes by your name.

What next?

Perhaps you are thinking that all this human being stuff falls into the nice-to-have-but-not-essential category of management. If you are, then I see your point. Most organisations have survived quite nicely without paying heed to the human being nature of their employees. Why should they bother now?

CHAPTER 15

Reclaiming Our Status as Human Beings

There has never been a golden age when, in our dealings with others, we human beings have taken full account of our heart and computer nature. Despite its constant presence, walking beside us, shaping our lives, leading us on or holding us back, for most of us our inner self remains a little-known, shadowy figure to be understood by the psychotherapist but not by our own dear selves. It is clear that all the knowledge, sophistication and technology accumulated since the emergence of the first members of the human family six to seven million years ago have not tamed the unruly nature of our core needs. Yet, it is equally clear that we have developed the capacity to do so. Evolution has given us a brain capable of reflection, awareness and imagination. We can work with ideas as well as concrete facts. We can label emotions, register them when they occur and interpret their impact upon us. Over the past century, we have developed a knowledge base in psychology, neuroscience, sociology and anthropology that can explain how our thinking and feeling structures develop and influence individual lives and societies. As I hope you will have realised from this book, we don't need to be scientists or therapists to make use of this knowledge because the basic principles on which we operate are not complex. In short, we have the tools to make better judgements about, and responses to, our true needs but do we have the will?

Throughout history, leaders, military and industrial, have sought to comprehend how to get the most from those under their span of influence. As our knowledge has become more refined, we have developed theories and approaches to shape the way people behave so that they deliver what organisations want. From Taylor's scientific management to Drucker's management by objectives[56] and onwards, at core, people have been regarded as cogs in a machine to be arranged, oiled occasionally, and then run efficiently to maximise the output of a system. In return, they were motivated not by the work itself but by a wage. Part of this bargain was that the cogs had little say in how they were used; they were just required to do their bit. What's more, all same-sized cogs were supposed to operate in the same way. Today, with our enlightened social conscience and its companion, legislation, we take more heed of the general welfare of people at work and our greater understanding of behaviour and motivation allows us to understand the impact of individual differences in performance. Of course, we still seek to shape what people do, albeit less by fixed work practices (unless you work in a call centre) and more by fixed processes of assessment and performance management. Whether our new ways of working really do recognise staff, employees, colleagues and bosses as 'human beings' rather than cogs is, however, another matter.

As an example, let's take the term *human resource*. What the term *human resource* really means is that there are people (leaders) and there are other people (staff). Staff are a resource to the leaders. They are the pairs of hands to be ordered and managed to fulfil the objectives of the senior team. It is little wonder, therefore, that where people are seen as a resource, close to objects, consideration of them as unique human beings falls a long way behind. One has to wonder, too, that if it's always been that way, does it matter and, if it does, is there any hope of change?

There's no escape from the human being in us all

One reason for taking greater cognisance of the human element at work is that ignoring it won't make it go away. Human being issues impact on performance. The question is whether leaders and managers make these issues work in the organisation's favour or whether valuable energy and resources are used trying to constrain them.

Human beings are the organisation: People often talk about the organisation in which they work as if it is a single entity. As if its senior management team is the 'brain' and the workforce are the 'muscles' to deliver what the brain decides and somewhere, in the overall ethos of the place, there is a heart that cares. But organisations are collectives. They don't have a heart. They don't stay up late at night worrying. They don't care and they don't love. They can't. Organisations, as entities, aren't human. Neither are they machines. Technology may be central to many businesses and public-sector enterprises but we can't ignore that, without people to operate it, there is no organisation. On this basis, it doesn't make logical sense to talk of people as a resource, a form of capital or an asset. The organisation is a system made up of people. The organisation is people.

Human beings bring their human qualities to work: If the organisation is people, it's alive and fizzing with the effects of both computer and heart. What an organisation becomes at any one point in time depends on how all the complex personalities within it, that's you and me, interact; like instruments in an orchestra, how we play together. As noted previously, when we go to work we don't leave our human selves at home, even if we try to. Any organisation is a maelstrom of human being concerns, our needs, our worries, our values, our beliefs, our skills and our behaviours. That might bring to mind images of ants scurrying around a nest or bees flying to and from their hive but we are not like insects following a pre-programmed course of action. We have the precious attribute of choice, which means that each of us has the opportunity to upset or uphold the welfare of our organisation. In 2013, one man, Edward Snowden,[57] succeeded in occupying the attention of the most senior members of numerous governments across continents. The rogue trader Nick Leeson single-handedly brought down the entire Barings Bank. The dominance of Fred Goodwin's personality nearly did the same for the Royal Bank of Scotland. And it's not just individual people with classified information or the most senior roles that make a difference. People are people wherever they are, however well or poorly paid, however skilled or challenged and, although those in power may make decisions that have the potential to create significant impact in an organisation, those in lowlier roles can do just the same by small, regular acts when they are carried out by an army of the many. While the Edward Snowdens and Nick Leesons of the world receive attention from the world's media for their behaviour, the myriad of unhelpful acts made by ordinary employees, each one a tiny injury to performance, may go completely unnoticed until all the small wounds amass to create a disabling gash.

'I' comes before 'we': As human beings, we bring attributes that enable people to work together harmoniously and with the best outcome for all. Compassion, humanity, determination, cooperation, curiosity, openness, sharing (you can create your own list) are among the many ways of living that we can bring to work and which will influence the way the whole enterprise chugs along. We can also bring attributes that, in general conversation, are regarded as 'not a good thing' but which seem to flourish in some organisations. Dominance, self-focus, 'I know best', authority through hierarchy, discrimination, exploitation, prejudice and disrespect, along with other even more unpleasant traits, can bubble along quite nicely in entities that, to the outside world, appear respectable and successful.

The difference between these two lists is the emphasis placed on 'we' or 'I'; how much we care for our own interests versus the interests of other human beings. Our own interests, the 'I', are always with us and create a strong draw towards behaviour that serves 'I'. When left to our own devices, human beings are selfish, even you and me. We compete for our own interests to be met with whatever resources we have available. How much space we are prepared to leave for the needs of others is extremely variable.

Although in organisational life, the battle between 'I' and 'we' is usually hidden or, if obvious, is rarely acknowledged, it can have significant consequences. 'I' does not like losing territory to 'we', even though change often requires people to give ground. The tussle to 'win' takes time and energy away from the organisation's goals and is witnessed in office politics and questionable decision-making. Quite often, the organisation's purpose is diverted to meet the needs of a few, usually senior, 'I's.

The cascade of 'I': The process of setting strategy and devising operational plans involves, on the surface, complex business analysis thrashed out around the boardroom table. Present at these discussions but without a name badge, and seated directly behind everyone involved, are shadowy figures – the individual needs of the senior leaders involved (the 'I' of each person). In the top roles, these needs are usually quite pronounced for there is much to gain and much to lose. Consider a newly appointed CEO who initiates a change programme. Is this because the business needs major change or is it in part for more personal reasons – to prove to others that he's worth his large salary, to prove to himself that he can indeed do this high-pressured job, or maybe to win respect from colleagues who were once his peers? His motivation is likely to stem from a mixture of both overt and covert goals, and even the CEO himself may be blind to some of the latter.

As a result, the goals cascaded downwards from a senior team are a mixture of true business needs coupled with more personal needs. At the next level down, managers do the same thing. They tailor the goals they have received to meet both the overall business objectives for their area but also to meet their own 'I', what they need from these objectives (to keep my job, to gain recognition, to get a pay rise or bonus, to do better than my peers, to look good to the external market, to have an easy life, and so on). The manager on the receiving end then adds his own 'I' to this before passing it down again, leading to a veritable avalanche of 'I's. In simpler terms, self-interest is involved at every stage of the process.

Where, then, is there space for considering 'we', the needs of others, the team, the department, the organisation overall, clients, customers and suppliers? 'We' gets squeezed out pretty quickly when the pressure for 'I' is great. For example, how is it that, at the very time the PPI and LIBOR fixing scandals were being exposed in the banking sector, other illegal practices were taking hold (e.g. mis-selling of interest rate hedging products, the manipulation of foreign exchange rates), despite CEOs' insistence that cultures had changed, that 'we' (particularly the customer) would now come before 'I' (bankers' bonuses).

The rule of 'I' creates fertile ground for unhealthy competition, conflict, pain, loss of integrity, short-term thinking and because the impact of 'I' is like a bolder rolling down hill, picking up speed as it goes, ultimately it has the potential to fracture or destroy an organisation. This self-interest cannot be banished but it can be modified. By taking a more holistic view of human beings, allowing for both their computer and heart selves, by bringing 'I' versus 'we' matter into the open and by demonstrating that a plan that is the best for 'we' does not diminish individuals or mean their core needs will be neglected, it is possible to gain emotional and thinking engagement with a sound purpose for organisational success that suits all stakeholders.

A choice of arguments

In this book, I have argued that dealing with issues arising from our human being nature has been left in the 'too difficult' basket for too long. It's time that the true cost of this avoidance was acknowledged and here's why.

The economic 'computer' argument: Getting into the intricacies of human beings may seem the very opposite of good housekeeping. Creating another layer of complexity diverts attention away from an organisation's main objectives, doesn't it? And, as noted several times, listening, understanding and taking account of the individual nature of people eats up a considerable slice of time if it's not to be merely lip service. But perhaps this time is not simply a cost; it may well be a sound investment that pays back handsomely.

Consider the notion of waste. In the 1980s and 90s, business process re-engineering made us focus clearly on waste. We learned to differentiate between what added to a process and what detracted from it. We know now that we can reduce costs by cutting out unnecessary steps in a process and removing actions that conflict with the end goal – all are waste in terms of time, effort and resource. But, even when systems are engineered to the utmost efficiency, human beings still have the capacity to create waste when they seek to meet their own needs before the needs of the organisation, when what could be used towards the common goal is used for personal need.

We waste time and effort and resources:

- *when we feel unsafe* as our attention will be centred on gaining our security. Fear can make us work hard but it may also prevent us experimenting with new or more creative ways of working. It can make us physically sick, leaving our desks empty and unproductive. Insecurity can make us behave as a block in the system (as in a middle manager 'concrete layer'). Fear can keep our heads down, following procedures and filling in the paperwork, keeping safe, while avoiding the true purpose of our work.

- *when we feel uncertain about our value or know that we are undervalued*; we're likely to focus our attention and time on seeking out evidence that will prove our worth, often disrupting the performance of others in the process. We might make decisions that impact across a vast section of an organisation just to show what we can do, whether the organisation truly needs it or not. Competition between peers may take precedence over the best result for the organisation. Being biggest or best may be of more importance than the end goal. Alternatively, we might do the opposite and avoid challenges because we fear further evidence of failure.

- *when we are not sure if we belong*; our communication will be limited, our relationships will be cautious or overly demanding and our trust in others will be low. If we overidentify with one group, we will downplay or ignore the needs of other teams and potentially block change.

- *when we feel stuck, bored and underused*; we will find
  entertainment elsewhere 'on work time' through long
  lunchtimes or 'pulling sickies' or keeping YouTube
  up and running or just doing whatever we like.
  Alternatively, we might introduce change because it's
  interesting, stimulating, exciting and because we can,
  rather than we should. Or we might just find a new
  place to work altogether.

- *when the purpose of work isn't clear*; we create
  waste through the reinvention of the organisational
  wheel, the regular restructurings, senior development
  programmes, values programmes, and initiatives that
  get repeated under a different name with each change
  of senior management.

- *when the question 'why' is addressed at a surface level
  only*; we may never get to the root of problems or
  address the real issues affecting performance, leaving
  them to rear their ugly heads time and time again.

Waste of this type is expensive and it's found at all levels
of an organisation. Its costs include loss of profit, loss of
reputation and loss of morale and some of these losses can
prove irreversible. Where personal interest is met in the wrong
way, where some human beings win and too many lose, where
it detracts from the performance of the organisation, when it
threatens sustainability, then this cost is too high.The 2015
Gallup survey of employee engagement in the US[58] (defined as
people being involved in, enthusiastic about and committed to
their work and workplace) found that, of over 80,000 people,

only 32% regarded themselves as engaged with their work while half, 50%, regarded themselves as not engaged. This represents a staggering degree of disengagement, particularly as the levels have changed little since 2000. Gallup's worldwide survey of 2013,[59] which included organisations from 142 countries, found the overall level of engagement to be an extraordinarily low 13%. By 2017 there had been only a marginal improvement to 15%.[60] Does this matter? It certainly appears to. Organisations in the top 25% of Gallup's engagement database have significantly higher productivity, profitability and customer ratings, less turnover and absenteeism and fewer safety incidents than those in the bottom 25%. Gallup estimate that in the UK actively disengaged employees cost the country between £52 billion and £70 billion per year.

Engagement, however, is considerably more important than just another indicator of performance. It may be a critical requirement for organisational survival.[61] In our new world, leaders and managers must grapple with the implications brought by a non-stop stream of change in their environment, change over which they have no direct control. The top-down, command-based management practices of the past, which emphasised looking inwards, controlling and refining internal practices and responding to change after the event, are unlikely to keep an entity in business now. To survive in today's world, the collective body of an organisation has to be curious, open-minded, willing to learn, collaborative and flexible. These attributes are essential if it is to have foresight, to anticipate what may lie ahead and to be sufficiently fleet of foot to keep pace with the changing nature of its environment. To succeed, these characteristics cannot be vested in a management team only. To be truly a learning organisation, the thinking, creativity, determination and energy of all employees has to be engaged. Instead of cogs or pairs of hands, employees at all levels must become part of the process through which an organisation is led. What's more, that's what employees will expect.

The teenagers of today will grow to become workers who are used to instant access to information, to being permanently connected to others wherever they are in the world, and where the boundary between work and non-work is fudged because they are always accessible ('always on'), whenever, wherever, across a wide range of devices.[62] They will be able to reach out across the world, beyond the limits of their own organisation, to build networks and friendships and to solve problems. Their world will be one in which those who once held power by virtue of the information they guarded will become disempowered as that information is available to all at a flick of a switch.

The young people who have benefited from previous generations' access to education and increased prosperity will be in a better position to get what they want from work. They will expect to be engaged, consulted and stimulated and will be able to identify whether work fulfils their personal purpose. They will want or even demand a variety of rewards in exchange for their labour, not just monetary payment. And, if dissatisfied, they will easily discover opportunities elsewhere and be ready to jump ship however many times is needed to meet their needs. An increase in self-employment and a decrease in organisational loyalty will require managers to be vigilant if they are to hold on to the skilled employees they need. This isn't just fanciful thinking. It's the stuff of work today for those who have the skills and potential that are in demand. For these individuals, the powerbase of the employment contract is shifting.

Yet, while technology is driving this change at an ever-increasing speed, human evolution is a slow process. A very slow process.

The employees of tomorrow will be the same, at their core, as the people who lived by candlelight, tilled the fields with horse-drawn ploughs and went to bed when the sun went down. Whatever technological advances the world throws at us, and however our work practices change as a result, our basic human nature does not alter. Our human being self has not changed. Hence, to engage the talented and skilled people they need, managers will have to be significantly better versed in understanding and working with this nature and more attuned to meeting human needs than they have in the past. Understanding how human beings tick is fast becoming a necessity for organisational survival, not just an interesting little diversion from the real business of making money.

But what about those whose talents and skills are not quite so much in demand? What does this information and communication rich world have in store for them? The rise in atypical contracts (fixed-term, zero-hours, part-time, agency workers etc.) suggests that they are increasingly becoming regarded as a disposable commodity. As such, their needs as human beings are of little interest to an organisation that pays for their services but has no concern for their working arrangements. The gap between feted employees and the 'commodity pairs of hands' workers risks growing wider still and, while this gap has always existed, is it the type of division we want to strengthen and carry forward? If we do, the cost will not be borne just by the individuals concerned, of whom there are many. It will lead to yet more waste of the valuable energy and thinking of many human beings. Creativity and insight are not a function of a role or level. They come with the whole human being package but they can't surface unless given the opportunity to do so. Enthusiasm isn't a function of a role. It's the result of being allowed to contribute to something worthwhile. Everyone who is part of an enterprise has the potential to contribute to moving it forward if the organisation allows them to do so. Beyond this waste of potential, there is also significant danger. The growing gap between those who are more and those who are less in demand also risks large numbers of disaffected people acting against the interests of an organisation; if you treat me unfairly then I may well do likewise. As mentioned before, employees don't have to occupy senior positions to do significant damage.

In contrast, imagine a place of work where everyone concerned is excited about the business of the organisation. Where everyone is looking for ways in which their role, whatever it is, adds to the glorious whole. That's an organisation that performs, creates and flexes with changing demands. It's an organisation with a good chance at survival and where all gain.

The moral, 'heart' argument: My computer-self generated the logical reasons just recounted to support a more rounded approach to human beings in the workplace but my heart-self tells me that I shouldn't need to do this. Is the aim of improving the satisfaction of human beings, of making our workplaces and society based on more of a 'we' than 'I' culture, not a desirable ambition in its own right? In a world where the difference between the haves and have-nots continues to increase, our workplaces risk amplifying inequality rather than championing our fundamental similarities. Like the emperor's retinue in the wonderful story *The Emperor's New Clothes* by Hans Christian Andersen,[63] we have come to believe in what we are told and not what we see. We accept argument at its face value, as rational thinking, without seeing the personal motivation beneath it.

Pseudo-logic can be heard all around us when apparently rational argument is used to mask personal and emotional need. Nowhere is this more evident than in the arguments given for senior executive pay and bonuses. The view that the few people who earn mega salaries are indispensable, that they have skills and abilities that others do not, is simply untrue. I know this. I have assessed many such people. Those who get to the top are certainly able. Whether they are irreplaceable I doubt. In 1998, the average FTSE 100 CEO was paid forty-seven times the salary of their average employee. By 2012, it had grown to a multiple of 133.[64] Talent and potential exist in all sectors of society yet we insist in looking for it in familiar places without exploring further. The argument that this level of remuneration is needed to attract the best is simply invalid if we haven't looked wider afield to find the best. Similarly, we have come to accept as truth that those whose job involves working with large sums of money are entitled to receive large sums in remuneration, almost regardless of the level of skill required.[65] The same thinking applied to those who work in a chocolate factory would lead to a pay packet stuffed with chocolate. Doctors and nurses should receive extra health and longer lives. This is nonsense, of course, but the pseudo-logic supporting excessive pay levels in the financial institutions and elsewhere doesn't make sense either. Where people are involved, there will always be 'I' and 'we'. Some will gain and some will lose but it's time to question the scale of this difference and the apparent rationale on which it is based.

Beyond pay, the moral argument requires us to consider whether it's acceptable that so many people spend much of their time involved in activities they actively dislike or feel neutral about. Is that the height of our ambition as a society? Is that what you want for yourself or for your children?

It's time to acknowledge human behaviour for what it is, in work and elsewhere. Human beings are capable of good and bad. By being willing to address what drives us and what we need to be at our best, we will not magically create a warm and cosy world. Good and bad will still exist but at least we will have the opportunity to foster more of the good and to be more proactive in identifying and dealing with the bad. If we have the will, we can enable people to feel more satisfied, happier even, about the activity which absorbs much of their waking hours – work.

So, am I supposed to change the world?

Not the big world. That would be a tad ambitious. How about starting with something smaller.

Imagine an organisation to be like a town drawn on a map. As we magnify the map, the streets, parks and lakes become visible. As we magnify it further, the individual plots of land become clear. If you get the right map, you can even see the deed numbers on each plot, identifying who owns each parcel of land. I know the deed number for my house and garden. That's my domain, where I live out my life each day. I know there are things I can do here and things I can't. I can design the flowerbeds just how I like them. I can put down decking and create arbours but if I try lighting a bonfire on a sunny day I won't get away with it. My neighbours will be at my door promptly asking me to put it out. I also have restrictions about what I can build in my garden. A shed's ok. A bigger building is not. Consider that as a manager in an organisation you have a plot of land, your own backyard. There are boundaries that you may not be able to cross. There are other plots that you have contact with and there are those further afield that may be harder to reach. In the privacy of your backyard, you can design and run your garden with a fair degree of freedom within the limits of your budget and the tools and manpower available. What will mark your garden out as different from the surrounding others will be the ambition you hold for the land. Even if all you have is a rusty spoon, you can make a difference. You have the scope to choose how your backyard operates.

In work, few managers are powerless. You may have a hard time working against a difficult culture or achieving pressing demands or dealing with unpleasant individuals but you are not without authority and you use your power each day. If you manage people, you influence their work life. You influence them as human beings, restricting or freeing them to give of their best. By recognising how both your heart and your computer influence the way you work, by acknowledging and understanding your own needs, then applying your good computer brain to understand your people, you can make the small changes needed to lift performance and make work a better place to live life. It's not within your gift to make the best life possible for other people but, within your own backyard, you can make a small contribution towards it. Both your heart and computer should agree with that.

What next?

Well that's down to your good human being self.

References and Notes

1. Reeves, M., Levin, S. & Ueda, D. (2016) The biological impact of corporate survival. *Harvard Business Review*, Jan–Feb, 46–55.

2. De Geus, A. (2002) *The Living Company*. Boston: Harvard Business Review Press, p3.

3. Kahneman, D. (2011) *Thinking, Fast and Slow*. New York: Farrar, Strauss and Giroux.

4. Bauer, P.J. & Larkina, M. (2014) Childhood amnesia in the making: different distributions of autobiographical memories in children and adults. *Journal of Experimental Psychology: General*, 143(2), 597–611.

5. Brown, J. (1964) *Flat Stanley*. New York: Harper & Row.

   In this children's story, the main character, Stanley Lambchop had the misfortune to be flattened. Although he enjoys the benefits of existing in his flat state, slipping under doors and travelling by envelope, he eventually becomes frustrated because he cannot live life as a full human being.

6. Goleman, D. (1995) *Emotional Intelligence: Why It Can Matter More Than IQ*. New York: Bantam Books.

7. McFarlane, A. (2010) The long-term cost of traumatic stress; intertwined physical and psychological consequences. *World Psychiatry*, 9(1), 3–10.

8. Gendron, M., Roberson, D., van der Vyver, J.M. & Barrett, L.F. (2014) Cultural relativity in perceiving emotion from vocalizations. *Psychological Science*, 25, 911–920.

9. Taylor, F. (1911) *The Principles of Scientific Management*. New York and London: Harper & Brothers.

10. *The UK Contact Centre HR & Operational Benchmarking Report 2016–17* (6th edition). ContactBabel.

11. Sardino, K. (2005) Behavioral genetics and child temperament. *Journal of Developmental and Behavioral Pediatrics*, 26(3), 214–223.

12. Competency and competency frameworks. CIPD Factsheet. (2017) Available at: https://www.cipd.co.uk/knowledge/fundamentals/people/performance/competency-factsheet#6374 [accessed November 2017)

    'In the past, HR professionals have tended to draw a clear distinction between "competences" and "competencies". The term "competence" (competences) was used to describe what people need to do to perform a job and was concerned with effect and output rather than effort and input. "Competency" (competencies) described the behaviour that lies behind competent performance, such as critical thinking or analytical skills, and described what people bring to the job. More recently however, there has been growing awareness that job performance requires a mix of behaviour, attitude and action and the terms are now more often used interchangeably.'

13. Microsoft announces pilot program to hire people with autism. *Microsoft on the Issues* [web blog], 3 April 2015. Available at: http://blogs.microsoft.com/on-the-issues/2015/04/03/microsoft-announces-pilot-program-to-hire-people-with-autism [accessed October 2015].

14. Crawley, B., Pinder, R. & Herriot, P. (1990) Assessment centre dimensions, personality and aptitude. *Journal of Occupational Psychology*, 63(3), 211–216.

15. Pittenger, J. (1993) Measuring the MBTI... and coming up short. *Journal of Career Planning & Placement*, 54(1), 48–52.

16. Crump, R. (3 August 2015) EY overhauls post-education recruitment selection process. *Accountancy Age*. Available at: http://www.accountacyage.com/aa/news/2420325/ey-overhauls-post-education-recruitment-selection-process [accessed October 2015].

    From 2016, EY no longer screens candidates based on academic results. Their final decision takes into account performance in all aspects of the selection process. At the early stages, the strongest candidates are identified using a new suite of situational strengths and numerical tests.

17. Jung, C.G. (1930) The stages of life. In: Read, H.E., Fordham, M.E. & Adler, G. (eds), *The Collected Works of C.G. Jung* (8), p771. Princeton: Princeton University Press.

'The nearer we approach to middle life, and the better we have succeeded in entrenching ourselves in our personal attitudes and social positions, the more it appears as if we had discovered the right course and the right ideals and principles of behaviour. For this reason, we suppose them to be eternally valid, and make a virtue of unchangeably clinging to them... Many – far too many – aspects of life which should also have been experienced lie in the slumber-room among the dusty memories; but sometimes, too, they are glowing coals under grey ashes.'

18. Moss. R. (2015) One-third using psychometrics have no training, finds survey. *Personnel Today*. Available at: https://www.personneltoday.com/hr/one-third-using-psychometrics-training-finds-survey [accessed October 2015]

19. Xu. F. & Kushnir. T. (2013) Infants are rational constructive learners. *Current Directions in Psychological Science*, 22, 28–32.

20. Horney, K. (1950) *Neurosis and Human Growth*. New York: W.W. Norton.

21. Maslow, A.H. (1943) A theory of human motivation. *Psychological Review*, 50(4), 370–396.

22. Cooper, C., Pandey, A. & Campbell Quick, J. (2015) *Downsizing: Is Less Still More?* Cambridge: Cambridge University Press.

23. Francis, R. (February 2015) *Freedom to Speak Up Review Report*. An independent review into creating an open and honest reporting culture in the NHS. Available at: http://webarchive.nationalarchives.gov.uk/20150218150512/http://freedomtospeakup.org.uk/the-report [accessed February 2016].

24. Harley, N. (September 2017) 'Bullying' Tesco executives falsified profits to boost salaries in scam which wiped £2bn off firm's value, court hears. *The Telegraph*. Available at: http://www.telegraph.co.uk/news/2017/09/29/bullying-senior-tesco-executives-falsified-profits-scam-boost [accessed September 2017].

25. Health and Safety Executive (2016) *Work Related Stress, Anxiety and Depression Statistics in Great Britain*. Available at: www.hse.gov.uk/statistics [accessed January 2017).

26. Wiedenfeld, S., Badura, A., Levine, S., O'Leary, A., Brown, S. & Raska, K. (1990) Impact of perceived self-efficacy in coping with stressors

on components of the immune system. *Journal of Personality and Social Psychology*, 59(5),1082–1094.

27. Kerr, R. & Robinson, S. (2012) Symbolic violence to economic violence: the globalizing of the Scottish banking elite. *Organization Studies*, 33(2), 247–266.

28. Confederation of British Industry (CBI) (2014) *Fit For Purpose: Absence and Work Based Health Work Survey, 2013*. London: Confederation of British Industry.

29. Willis Eighth Annual Health and Productivity Survey report (April 2014). Available at: https://www.willis.com/documents/ publications/Services/Employee_Benefits/FOCUS_2014/20140402 50074 HCP Health Prod FINAL V2.pdf [accessed June 2016]

30. European Agency for Safety and Health at Work (2012) *Motivation for Employers to Carry Out Workplace Health Promotion - literature review*. Luxembourg: Publications Office of the European Union.

31. Cancer Statistics (2017). Macmillan Cancer Support. Available at https://www.macmillan.org.uk/about-us/what-we-do/evidence/ cancer-statistics.html#260408 [accessed November 2017]

32. Macmillan Cancer Support. *Cured - But at What Cost?* (July 2013). Available at: https://www.macmillan.org.uk/documents/cancerinfo/ livingwithandaftercancer/consequences/cured-but-at-what-cost-report. pdf [accessed November 2017].

33. Scarborough, P, Wickramasinghe, K., Bhatnagar, P. & Rayner, M. (2011) *Trends in Coronary Heart Disease 1961-2011*. London: The British Heart Foundation, p4.

34. CIPD (July 2016) *Employee Outlook: Mental Health in the Workplace*. London: CIPD.

35. Sainsbury Centre for Mental Health (2007) *Mental Health at Work: Developing the Business Case*. London: Sainsbury Centre for Mental Health.

36. Financial Services Authority (December 2011) The Failure of the Royal Bank of Scotland Board Report. FSA: London.

37. Belonging in this sense means 'feeling part of', not 'being owned by'.

38. Rotter, J.B. (1966) Generalized expectancies for internal versus external control of reinforcement. *Psychological Monographs: General & Applied*, 80(1), 1–28.

39. Bandura, A. (1997) *Self-efficacy: The Exercise of Control*. New York: W.H. Freeman.

40. Conversano, C., Rotondo, A., Lensi, E., Vista, O. D., Arpone, F. & Reda, M.A. (2010) Optimism and its impact on mental and physical well-being. *Clinical Practice & Epidemiology in Mental Health*, 6, 25–29.

41. Bolier, L., Haverman, M., Westerhof, G., Riper, H., Smit, F. & Bohlmeijer, E. (2013) Positive psychology interventions: a meta-analysis of randomized controlled studies. *BMC Public Health*, 13, 119.

42. Seligman, M., Steen, T., Park, N. & Peterson, C. (2005) Positive psychology progress: Empirical validation of interventions. *American Psychologist*, 60(5), 410–421.

43. Strandh, M., Winefield, A., Nilsson, K. & Hammarström, A. (2014) Unemployment and mental health scarring during the life course. *European Journal of Public Health*, 24(3), 440–445.

44. Mann, S. (2007) Boredom at work. *The Psychologist*, 20, 90–93.

45. Hurst, A. (2014) *The Purpose Economy*. Boise: Elevate.

46. *Scottish Widows Savings Report*, 2014.

47. Miller, J. (2011) Sustainable Organisation Performance. What Really Makes the Difference. A Shaping the Future Report. CIPD: London

48. Hafenbrack, A., Kinias, Z. & Barsade, S. (2014) Debiasing the mind through meditation, mindfulness and the sunk-cost bias. *Psychological Science*, 25(2), 369–376.

49. Harvard Business Review Analytic Services report (2015) *The Business Case for Purpose*. Harvard Business School Publishing. Available at: http://www.ey.com/Publication/vwLUAssets/ey-the-business-case-for-purpose/$FILE/ey-the-business-case-for-purpose.pdf [accessed January 2016].

50. Barry, L., Garr, S. & Liakopoulos, A. 'Performance management is broken. In: *Global Human Capital Trends 2014: engaging the 21st century workforce. A report by Deloitte Consulting LLP and Bersin by Deloitte*. Deloitte University Press. Available at: https://documents.dupress.deloitte.com/HCTrends2014 [accessed January 2017].

51. Berne, E. (1964) *Games People Play*. New York: Grove Press Inc.

52. Gallup Report (2013) *State of the Global Workplace: Employee Engagement Insights for Business Leaders Worldwide*.

53. Musick. K & Meier, A. (2012) Assessing causality and persistence in associations between family dinners and adolescent well-being. *Journal of Marriage and the Family*, 74(3), 476–493.

54. Scullen. S, Mount, M. & Goff, M. (2000) Understanding the latent structure of job performance ratings. *Journal of Applied Psychology*, 85(6), 956–970.

55. Buckingham, M. & Goodall, A. (April 2015) Reinventing Performance Management. Harvard Business Review. Available at: https://hbr.org /2015/04/reinventing-performance-management [accessed January 2016].

56. Drucker, P. (1954) *The Practice of Management*. New York: Harper & Brothers.

57. In 2013, Edward Snowden, a computer contractor with the CIA, leaked intelligence information to the press before absconding to Russia.

58. Adkins, A. (January 2016) Employee Engagement in U.S. Stagnant in 2015. *Gallup news website*. Available at: http://news.gallup.com/ poll/188144/employee-engagement-stagnant-2015.aspx [accessed October 2016].

59. Gallup report (2013) *The State of The Global Workforce. Employee Engagement Insights for Business Leaders Worldwide*.

60. Emond, L. (August 2017) 2 Reasons why employee engagement programs fall short. *Gallup News website*. Available at: http:// news.gallup.com/opinion/gallup/216155/reasons-why-employee-engagement- [accessed December 2017].

61. Vielmetter, G. & Sell, Y. (2014) *Leadership 2030*. New York: AMACOM.

62. Morgan, J. (2014) *The Future of Work*. New Brunswick: John Wiley & Sons.

63. Hans Christian Andersen, (1837) The Emperor's New Clothes, in *Fairy Tales Told for Children*, Reitzel, C. A. Copenhagen.

64. The High Pay Centre (December 2013) *One Law For Them: How Big Companies Flout Rules on Executive Pay*. Available at http:// highpaycentre.org/pubs/one-law-for-them-how-big-companies-flout-rules-on-executive-pay [accessed January 2016].

65. Salz, A. (2013) *Salz Review: An Independent Review of Barclays' Business Practices*. London: Barclays PLC, p9.

   The 2013 Salz Review into the Barclays LIBOR scandal noted, 'We concluded that the reputational problems for Barclays stem in part from the perception that, at least in the UK, some bankers have appeared oblivious to reality. In the eyes of many stakeholders, despite the banks' role in the financial crisis (and the consequent recession), despite billions of pounds of liquidity support from taxpayers, many senior bankers seemed still to be arguing that they deserved their pre-crisis levels of pay (levels that were in any circumstances incomprehensible to the general public).'

Printed in Poland
by Amazon Fulfillment
Poland Sp. z o.o., Wrocław